SPEAKING FOR THEMSELVES

*Hearing the Gospel
from the dispossessed,
the undervalued
and the marginalized*

CLIFFORD A.S. ELLIOTT

D1604437

Abingdon Press
Nashville

Speaking for Themselves:
Hearing the Gospel from the Dispossessed, the Undervalued, and the Marginalized

ISBN 0-687-39165-2

Library of Congress Catalog Number: 90-42537

CONTENTS

As the hart longs
for flowing streams,
so longs my soul
for thee, O God.
My soul thirsts for God,
for the living God.
When shall I come and behold
the face of God?
My tears have been my food
day and night,
while people say to me continually,
"Where is your God?"

These things I remember,
as I pour out my soul...
Why are you cast down, O my soul,
and why are you disquieted within me?
Hope in God; for I shall again praise God,
my help and my God.

My soul is cast down within me,
therefore will I remember thee...
Deep calls to deep
at the thunder of thy cataracts;
all thy waves and thy billows
have gone over me.
By day the Lord commands God's steadfast love;
and at night God's song is with me,
a prayer to the God of my life.

(From Psalm 42, Revised Standard Version, adapted)

ACKNOWLEDGEMENTS

There is not room to mention all the people who made this book possible. The McGeachy Senior Scholarship of the United Church of Canada helped by granting me a generous scholarship to do the necessary research. The McGeachy committee not only supported me during the period of research but gave me great freedom in the way I pursued it. The Jackman Foundation provided funds to purchase a word processor. Jim Sanderson's assistance and endless patience were invaluable as I struggled with the mysteries of this new technology.

Throughout the research and writing I received help from many mentors. Chief among these was Dr. Terry Anderson of the Vancouver School of Theology. During the year I spent at V.S.T., Terry gave most generously of his time, met with me every week, suggested reading, guided me toward a focus and, best of all, regularly got me enthusiastic about the project. After I returned to Toronto, I met with him every few months, during which time he continued to guide me. Dr. David Lochhead of V.S.T. also met with me frequently. I appreciated his keen theological insight and his sensitivity to the human struggle. I am also grateful to V.S.T. for giving me an office and a warm welcome to their community.

In Toronto, Wilfred Cantwell Smith, well known scholar of world religions, gave me encouragement at a crucial moment in my thinking. Sr. Margaret Brennan of Regis College shared her deep spirituality and her genuine love of ordinary people and their stories. Roger Hutchison of Emmanuel College helped me to think more clearly about what I was trying to do. Many others of the Emmanuel faculty also gave generously of their time and interest, and the college provided a much-appreciated office to work in.

At St. Andrew's College, Saskatoon, where I was pastor-in-residence for a semester, I was invited to use some of the material in this book in discussions with the faculty and students. I was pleased to see how valuable such research can be in many aspects of theological education. A wonderful bonus of being in Saskatoon was my friend, David Carpenter. He is a writer who teaches English at the University of Saskatchewan, and he provided another perspective, gave suggestions and cheered me on my way.

I took advantage of many friends and colleagues, who read drafts of single chapters of the book and gave me their comments and advice. Unfortunately, there are too many to list their names. They were valuable as early editors, and in their genuine faith in what I was trying to do. Without them, I would have floundered even more than I did.

Special thanks are due to the people who introduced me to the persons I interviewed. Without them I would never have been able to meet most of the wonderful people who told me their stories, and without their personal recommendation the people could hardly have welcomed me as they did or been as open as they were.

The nature of the research was not quantitative, so I did not interview a large number of people. I want to thank the more than 30 people, from Vancouver Island to Labrador, who agreed to be interviewed and were often enthusiastic about it. I could not have believed that people, in the space of an hour or two, would reveal so much of their personal history and experience. All of them agreed without reservation to have their stories used, although I have changed the names of all those whose stories are in this book. There was not room to include their entire stories, but the words printed here are essentially their words.

Most of all, I want to thank my wife, Mary Sanderson, who urged me to undertake the project, and who became as interested in it as I was. She, too, read the chapters, made suggestions and never slackened in her excitement about the purpose and value of the undertaking.

AUTHOR'S NOTE
When quoting scripture, I have used three versions: the Authorized Version, the Revised Standard Version, and the New English Bible. Where the quotation is very brief, it did not seem necessary to identify the particular book, chapter and verse. In some cases, there have been slight adaptations to make the language more inclusive.

This book is dedicated to Marlene, Don, Donna, Lorne, Jennifer, Nora, Bob and Aunt Bessie, who are the real authors of this book.

INTRODUCTION

This is not the kind of book I started to write. I wanted to write a book that would make faith more simple and real and more accessible to a wider group of people. After more than 40 years as a minister in a variety of congregations, I had become concerned that the way we proclaimed our message made it unintelligible or irrelevant to most people outside the church, and probably to a good many inside the church, and perhaps – perish the thought – even to some of us who were proclaiming it!

I had few doubts about the essential message, if only it could be expressed in ordinary, contemporary language and with the use of everyday illustrations and applications. I felt that the language, metaphors and symbols that had been developed in another day and in another situation continued to be used even though they did not belong to our day. What does it mean, for example, to say that "Jesus Christ died on the cross to save us from our sins"? Or to ask people to "accept the Lord Jesus Christ as their personal savior"? What do the words "repentance," "conversion," "salvation," mean? For that matter, what do we mean by "God"?

The Bible still may be widely read, but large sections of it mean little or nothing to the average reader. I wanted to acknowledge all that, and also to acknowledge that the Christian church in the Western world has consisted mostly of middle-class people who have, to a degree we fail to realize, shaped religion to their own culture. That has had the effect not only of dangerously identifying Christianity with middle-class culture but of excluding people of other cultures from whatever good news we have to offer.

I thought I would reach out to people outside the church to discover new ways of communicating and understanding the Gospel. I decided to interview a variety of people, mostly from outside the church, in order to learn the language, metaphors and symbols they used. Then I would try to translate the Christian message into their terms. I soon realized, however, that this approach had the weakness of some of the old missionary styles. It does go to the trouble of learning other people's languages, but only to communicate our message to them. It assumes that the only art we have to learn is that of communication.

There is something very condescending about this process. It is the one we used to a large degree when we sent missionaries to Canada's native peoples. It assumed that they had no religion of their own and that we had to fill a large spiritual vacuum, or that what religion they did have was false and had to be *expelled or corrected. Often it also assumed that in order to be Christians they would have to learn to speak English and stop speaking their own language. They were supposed to become like us. All too late, we are realizing how much we have to learn from them, especially in such things as reverence for the environment and our unity with nature. All too late, we are repenting of the serious wrongs we did in the name of religion.*

The fault was that we had been thinking of a one-way communication instead of a two-way conversation. I saw my task as listening to people not primarily in order to learn their language but to hear what they had to say to us. So all I did was ask people to tell me their life story and how they coped with difficulties and challenges along the way. I did not prepare any questionnaire. I simply recorded their stories, transcribed them, then pored over them. Then I asked, "What can we learn from this life, from what this person has discovered?"

Very few of the people I talked with had read any theology. They were, however, people who had lived – and were living – difficult lives, and had come up with some real questions and, in some cases, real answers. Or, if not answers, at least ways of coping with the questions, which may be a more profound thing in the long run. Most of them might be regarded by middle-class people as "marginalized." But that is a dangerous word to use: a person who is "mainstream" in one context may well be "marginalized" in another.

I found that, when asked to tell their story, most of them talked about their childhood and whether it was happy or unhappy. Many of them had been abused in one way or another and still bore the marks of that abuse. Many had rebelled against the things they were taught or expected to accept as children, things they felt restricted their development or left them feeling guilty, even about attitudes and actions they now feel are good and right. They had had a hard time forgiving themselves and extending forgiveness to those who had harmed them.

Their rebellion against their past and their painful frustration with their continuing self-rejection led some of these people to a kind of turning point in their lives. We might call it a conversion.

All the people whose stories I have chosen for this book have suffered greatly. Some have lived through poverty and hard times. One suffers a profound depression that will not go away. Some have had periods of illness of other kinds. One lost her only son in a drowning accident. Some have suffered inner pain as they agonized over difficult decisions or changes in their lives.

It is out of such struggles that these people have hewn a faith or way of coping with life. There is something real and down-to-earth about their faith. I find myself not only informed by it, but challenged. I cannot respond to such stories and such concrete faith with abstractions. I cannot shape their struggles into a doctrine that I then put alongside a creed or statement of faith that has been lifted out of its context. What these people believe is who they are.

My response to these people and their stories, I came to see, could not be an objective one. I must involve myself in their stories to try to feel what they feel. More than that, since they had told me the story of their lives so openly and honestly, did I not have to listen to my own story and try to discover what I have learned from it? I was impressed by the ability of these people to reflect on their lives and to articulate what they had discovered, what changes they had to make in their way of living. Could I do the same?

I decided to try. I would reflect on their stories, then try to relate their struggles to my own struggles and see what might evolve. It wasn't easy.

On the one hand, I feel that my life is very ordinary and that to talk about it or write about it is to be presumptuous – to imply that I have something unique or unusual to offer from my experience. On the other hand, if there is something about my life that is special, I don't want to talk about it. It is too personal, too sacred. However, if I were to value what others told me about their lives, there seemed no valid reason for me to withhold anything from my life. Otherwise, I would be a voyeur or an exploiter of their experiences. So I decided, as I reported their stories, to include, from time to time, portions of my own story.

The result has been a struggle. I have had to struggle with my story and with their stories. But I should not have been surprised by that. After all, in reading their stories I was deeply impressed, moved, sometimes appalled by what they went through, and in some cases are still going through. And in retrospect, I see that the crucial moments in my life have been times of struggle, too.

There was the struggle with the severe depression that struck the Canadian prairies in the thirties and left its mark on all our family with anxiety about money, the dashing of hopes, the search for ways to cope. There was the effort to rework my faith, from something I felt to be rather narrow to something that could relate to a wider context. There was the wrestling with the birth of our handicapped daughter and how to explain it or at least to accept it – and then, after I had accepted it, to accept her early death. There was the struggle with my wife's depressions, and later with her death. There was the anxiety about my approaching retirement when I felt my work to be so fulfilling. There was the struggle with the experience of ageing and the plain fact that death could come at any time.

Struggle. And yet I had found, as these people did, that struggle, while at times very painful, can be exciting, even exhilarating. That is because a person who struggles is not usually merely working with something but toward something. Not to struggle is to accept the status quo: to be a passive victim of life's circumstances. To struggle is to assert our humanity, to affirm our creativity, to express our hope and faith in a very concrete way. The ultimate struggle is with ourselves and with God. We all want security and peace of mind. But are we also not excited by the prospect of wrestling in an intensely intimate embrace with reality – with God's very self? Do we not have the feeling that that is the ultimate human experience and that out of it we could emerge transformed? Yes, like Jacob of old, even blessed?

I started to write a book from the church to people outside the church. Then I thought I might better let people outside the church speak to those like me who are inside it. Then I realized that these people are very much a part of the church, though it may not be the institutional church. Why not think of it as a conversation between people who belong to that larger church?

In this conversation we will hear people speaking in a language that is quite different from sophisticated middle-class language. Yet this very language is what jars us to look beneath our careful phrases, to ask what it is we are really saying. Sometimes we may find their language shocking, even obscene. I can only say that it did not seem obscene when they used it and that I had no sense that they were cursing or swearing as I might be if I used such language.

In any case, I hope that we may hear the good news of God's grace as they have heard it and have our own lives and faith enriched. I hope, too, that we may find a new appreciation for the sacredness of our own stories and see God at work in them.

MY STORY

As I listened to the people whose stories are in this book, I was forced, again and again, to think about my own life story. Living through their experiences with them led me to relive some of my experiences and to consider how they had affected me – helped shape my attitudes and my faith. From time to time, in commenting on their stories, I refer to experiences in my life. I often find a surprising similarity, despite the differences in our backgrounds. Since I do make these references to my life, let me tell you now a little of the events that seemed to me formative in my life.

I was born in 1919 in the village of Langham, Saskatchewan. I was the fourth of five children. My father was a businessman, selling cars and farm machinery in this agricultural region of the Canadian prairies. When the Depression of the 1930s struck, his business collapsed. He had to dissolve his partnership and dismiss his employees. It was a serious blow to him and to the rest of us, economically, emotionally and spiritually.

Our whole family was active in the local United Church, but my father was much drawn, during the Depression, to some evangelistic services held in a tent on a vacant lot across from our house. He and some others formed a new congregation in the village, although he continued to attend the United Church.

I was much influenced by my father and at the age of 14 had a conversion experience that was to affect my whole life. A few years later a student minister persuaded me to become a candidate for ministry, even though I was at that time somewhat disillusioned with the United Church.

At university in Saskatoon, and later at St. Andrew's Theological College in the same city, my faith changed and grew. In the summers, I served as a student minister, mostly in remote areas of northern Saskatchewan. Two years after graduation, I pursued post-graduate studies in New York City where my faith changed and grew again. I returned to Saskatchewan and served in a church in North Battleford, a place of about six thousand people. I had married just before going to graduate school, and in North Battleford my wife and I had two of our four children. My wife was a superb musician, and I had studied singing during my time at university, so music became a very important part of our home.

After five very happy years we moved to Hamilton, Ontario. There, my wife experienced the first of her serious depressions. We had two children there, including a child with Down's syndrome. This child was to profoundly influence our lives for many years.

Seven years later we moved to Edmonton, Alberta. It was the early sixties and the church was flourishing. My wife, however, was affected by the move and suffered another depression, though not as serious as the first, because better medical treatment had been developed. But her depressions caused her and the family great pain.

In 1966, we moved to Toronto, where I became minister of a downtown church in an area with many difficult social problems. My wife became caught up in the musical and artistic life of Toronto and seemed happier than she had been for many years. Later, when we moved to another church in Toronto she did not suffer the same emotional upheaval because she was able to continue her contacts and activities. However, in 1976 she developed cancer. After a mastectomy she was pronounced cured, but about a year later the cancer returned. She died the next year.

Meanwhile the children all left home except for Gracie, our Down's syndrome child. It was very difficult to provide an adequate home life for her, and after much research and many serious misgivings I placed her in a residence for mentally handicapped adults. She was about twenty years old but seemed more like a child of four or five. She had always had a heart condition, which threatened her life from the beginning, but we had learned to live with it. Very suddenly, just before her twenty-second birthday, she had a heart attack and was gone in a few minutes.

Seven years after my wife died I remarried, and soon afterward retired from the pastoral ministry. I was fortunate to receive a senior scholarship from the United Church to do research in the area of how better to communicate the Gospel. This book is one of the products of that research. I became a volunteer at a hospice for people with AIDS and served, as well, as a co-facilitator of a support group for relatives of people with AIDS. These experiences have had a significant effect on my life and enriched my retirement.

1

MARLENE
The Struggle With Our Childhood

Marlene works in a church-sponsored centre for the education and training of handicapped adults in Montreal. She is an attractive, plump woman in her mid-forties, with a round face and dark hair. She seems constantly to be smiling and she laughs easily, especially at herself. She has a winsome quality that comes from a rare combination of self-acceptance and an utter lack of affectation.

I was born in 1943 and lived most of my life till about 1966 in New Brunswick – moved there from Valleyfield, Quebec with my mother and stepfather. I didn't know he was my stepfather until I was 17 years old – we were seven children and I had two stepbrothers. My father was a bricklayer whenever he could find work, and we seemed to move from place to place constantly. My mother worked extremely hard – always took in laundry or did extra work trying to make money. We always had food and we never thought we were poor but we always had porridge and pancakes and codfish, and my mother always baked.

The sad part about our life, I think, is that my father was a bootlegger. We had no friends when we were kids. No families wanted their kids to play with us. At the time we didn't realize that was the problem. Nobody came out and said they couldn't play with us for that reason. We were constantly being harassed by people who came to the house. It was a thing we got used to – just thought it was a natural way to live. I was sexually abused by some of these people. As a child that is a hard thing to cope with. It went on from the time I was five until I was about thirteen – until a person tried to figure out that this was not the way to live. About that time my father got put in jail for bootlegging. And then we really had a hard time because there was no food at all. There was no social assistance or anything, and maybe the legion would bring us a box of groceries once a month. Between 13 and 17 life was still hard. When my father came back, as much as he was a bricklayer and there was a lot of work to be done, he just never stayed in a job very much. There was never any money – my mother still took in laundry and she opened up a small grocery store, which kept us in food but that was about it. A lot of people in that area

1

needed help and she just didn't say no if somebody needed something. So that was kind of a hard thing.

I got pregnant at 17. Got married before my son was born. My husband and I stayed with his parents, then we moved to Montreal. My son was mentally handicapped, and we came to Montreal knowing that it would be better, for more facilities were here for him and he'd be better looked after. He wasn't expected to live. We stayed here two years and moved back with his parents again. We stayed there a few more years, had three children more, moved to Montreal again because my oldest son was getting to school age and there were schools here. There wasn't any in New Brunswick.

Life was hard here. My husband worked some. We were on social assistance, and we never had enough food. Didn't know what it was like to go to the grocery store. I think I stayed in the house three years without going outside. I might have sat on the step but I didn't go to the store. I guess I wasn't expected to go. My husband took the money and he got the groceries. If he felt like buying booze he did, and that was it. I wasn't allowed to go. I was a battered wife. I guess I got knocked down more times than I stood up. I had another son while I was here – first a stillborn and then another son after that. My husband and I didn't get along very well and finally we separated in 1971. I was left with five children. The oldest was 10 and the youngest was 5.

I really didn't know what I was going to do. I hadn't done anything. I had had to stay home. I did what a housewife was supposed to do. I was really scared. I didn't think I would survive.

But then my son started to go to nursery school. Some people had asked, would I like him to go? So I started meeting some people and some people said, "Why don't you come and help us set the tables and do things like that and it will give you a change." Some of the kids were in school and it worked out well, so I did. Then some people asked me if I would like to work. Well, I just didn't know what to do. If I gave up my welfare cheque and had to work what was I going to do for the rent if something happened? Oh, my goodness! I didn't think I would survive doing that but anyway I went off welfare.

My oldest son at that time was having seven to eight seizures a day, and the school would phone and complain. I almost quit my job. But if I did that I would always be stuck on welfare and I didn't want that either. I was getting independent and I wanted that money. When I got my first few pay cheques I bought a fridge full of food and things I never had – an electric frying pan, a Mixmaster, a second-hand stove that had an oven – my goodness! – and then I bought things for the kids, like clothes they never had, gym outfits, running shoes ... I just couldn't believe I had money.

I was a cook. I used to cook the school lunch for 175 kids a day. I loved it. It was something I could do. I never knew I could do anything. I was told all my life, "You can't do anything – you'll never be able to work – you only went to Grade 9 – you don't speak very well – you don't know how to make conversation – when people talk to you you don't say anything – you're only good to stay home with the children." And I might as well get used to that – that was all I was good for. My husband used to tell me that all the time because he wanted me to stay at home and he wanted things to be ready so that when he came in for supper it would be on the table and you'd better not be late. When you're brought up that way – you're there for your husband and that's what you see all your life – you don't know any better. It was not a two-way bargain, for sure.

Now I work with mentally handicapped adults. It was strange how it happened. As I said, I was cooking for the school-lunch children. I have a mentally handicapped son who is 27 now but at the time would have been 19. They came and asked me if I would be interested in opening a program that would help other people in the area who had mentally handicapped adults at home and there were no facilities for them. I said, "Don't be so silly, I couldn't possibly do that. Look, I'm cooking, I couldn't possibly do that." And they said, "Look, you have that experience. You have a son. You're the one that brought him up, nobody was there to help you." I said, "Yes, but that's not like doing other children," and they said, "Yes, but look how you feel for your own son and how you always talk to other people about what their children should have." I said, "Yes, what they should have and what I have are two different things." Anyway, I said I would be willing to try it but I was so scared I couldn't believe I would do it.

We were just lucky that it was a great success. We have a long waiting list – there are a lot of people waiting to come in. But it's something we never know and my greatest fear is that one day my job will close and I don't know what I would do. I often wonder if I'll ever have to go back on welfare. That's my greatest fear. Because it's degrading – people have no self-worth when they're on welfare unless, of course, they want to be on welfare. You have people coming to your door checking up on you, looking in your fridge to see what kind of food you have, asking if you have somebody living with you, saying, "Do you mind your kids?" "How come you have a small radio?" which somebody gave you, or somebody gave you a second-hand TV – "How come you had that?" "Where did you get the money to buy that? Who bought that?" You aren't worth anything – your life isn't important. And if you had a clean house when they came in, well, that was something else. I mean, I don't know what they thought – we were supposed to live in a dirty house? I had no bathtub and no washing machine when I had all my children – I washed by hand. I had four children in diapers at one time and had to wash by hand. It was a hard thing. When I think about it today I wonder how I could do all those things because now, today, now that I'm working I think I'm so well off I can't believe it.

I think working with the handicapped – that's what keeps me going. That's what gives me a lift. Every day I have a reward. Every day they do something for me. How to cut their meat with a knife. Or, they might just say – one day I dropped something on the floor – and they say, "Marlene, you got the dropsy today?" And yet they never said a sentence in their life, but because they said that I was just so shocked. I was so happy I had a lift for a month. Or any other little thing they do. And they are so loving. They need the caring and I think I care – I give them that but they give it back to me and I don't feel my life's not worthwhile. I don't feel all I do is work, go home and work, look after my son, come back to work and do the whole thing. I have a family that I'm looking after here but they're looking after me, too – I'm not alone. They really care what happens to me. If I'm off one day sick they're really upset. They want to know, "Are you okay?" My other children do, too, but they have their own families. My daughter phones me to see how I am, of course. But there was still a little something that was missing.

Then I thought one day, I think a person waits for miracles all the time. I wanted a miracle because I thought I was punished when I had my oldest son because I got pregnant before I was married. You know the whole story, "God is punishing you, look out. He punished you, that's why you had that child. If you hadn't sinned before you were married you wouldn't have had a child like that." My mother was always very religious. She was Catholic. She always said that, I don't know how many times. So I guess I got to believe it after a while. It took me a long time to realize it wasn't true. God is not punishing me for that. But it took me a long time to realize that, too. I realized that wasn't true, and in many ways God did help me over the years.

And the other thing, talking about miracles, was that I was brought up to the belief there was a God and if there was a God why did he give me a son like that? That was a hard thing to live with – why would he punish me? So I got

4

pregnant, but other people do all kinds of things worse than that. And I was waiting for that big miracle – instantly he was going to make my son better. He'd say, "Marlene, okay, you tried to live a good life and I'll reward you for that." I waited for that. I waited and waited and waited for the miracle but then I realized that there is not going to be a big miracle. That's not going to happen. God's not going to come down and change all the world into people having enough to eat, no more welfare, rich people treating poor people right. That's not going to happen. But it took me a long time.

And I guess it was little things that I never considered were a miracle but they were. My son, as I said, had eight seizures a day from when he was 9 months old to when he was 17. We couldn't even go to the grocery store because he'd fall down and have a seizure. People would go by and say, "Look at that kid on dope. My God, doesn't his mother know any better?" Then suddenly last year, he was fine, he didn't have any. Now he's started having some little ones again but they're nothing compared to what he had.

Even finding that cure was a miracle. I think it was a miracle. I think it was a miracle, too, that I brought all my children up. There's lots of little things when you stop to think about them. The thing was I stopped waiting for the big miracle and saw the little good things. Anyway, I feel fine about it. It keeps me going.

In the place where I work we do some academic and training for independent living, and that depends on each person. It's sponsored by The United Church of Canada. Nobody is pushed out. And this is something that's really good. Before, people wanted a turnover. They would say, "Well, what are you doing? What's your turnover? How long have you been keeping so-and-so in your program?" We have 23 registered, we have 15 approximately come every day. There is myself and another woman who run this program and ours is a slow turnover. Suppose Mr. Brown phones up and he needs Billy, one of our students, to come in and do janitorial. We just don't take Billy and put him in to do janitorial. Mr. Brown has to work with him. We go and make sure that he's well suited. What I've learned is that mentally handicapped adults don't have much that's really important to them. But what they do have they're happy about and it's important to them. Why should we take it away from them? If they are happy with what we offer here, I'm happy to give it to them. I don't want to put them in a situation where they have no happiness at all.

Often we have church groups that come through and visit our program. A lot of money comes in from donations from different churches throughout the area. They often say, "Oh, you have a lot of patience." When you like your job and you really enjoy what you're doing I don't think it's patience. It's just like a family, like I said, something we want to do. And also it's something I enjoy doing, and I need it. They need it, but I need it also. I learn a lot of things from the people here. Caring is one thing. Loving's another. Understanding is the biggest thing I think I get. It's understanding because they can show me things I never thought possible.

I think I wore myself out the first year. Then after that we met in a group and we decided they are adults and some were functioning and we decided, "What would they like to do? How do they feel about what we do?" And they said sometimes they thought we treated them like babies, and they were right – we did. They were adults. When it's your child, you don't want him to grow up. I never wanted Richard to grow up. He was easier to look after when he was a child. He went to bed when I told him, he did what I told him. If we made spaghetti I gave it to him, he ate it. That's not fair. If you came here I wouldn't say to you, "Oh, here, eat this," or, "Time to do music," or go make your bed or watch TV or get ready for bed, and that's what I was doing.

They taught me if I was teaching them to be independent then why wasn't I teaching my own son to be independent? Why was I treating him like a baby? And I said, "But I'm not doing that." And they said, "Oh, sure you are. You don't let him go to work by himself, you have to bring him every day. Why don't you let him go by himself? But, oh, you're telling us it's all right if we go to work by ourselves – we shouldn't need anyone to help us down the street." And they were right. I did everything for him. I made his bed, I still cook his meals because I'm frightened of his seizures. But he's more independent now. They taught me a lot. We learned a lot from each other. They're still teaching me.

At our parents' meetings we talked a lot about why we have a retarded child and a lot of people believed God was punishing them. That was a surprise – I thought it was just me who used to feel like that. I think it helped me that they thought it was some kind of a punishment. They didn't know what they did. Some said, "I got a baby before I was married." The others thought they did something but they didn't remember exactly what would be that bad that they would get punished. Some said, "Why did it happen to us to have a retarded child because my husband and I, we have a good life, we go to church, we give our donation in, we do what's expected of us."

And they really couldn't understand that. I said, "I thought God, if he did give people a retarded child it's because he thought they really could look after them. Because not everybody could look after them. I used to feel like you and think that it was a burden and it was awful and I feel guilty about thinking that but I think God gave me my son because he was a special child – and I needed that special child to hold me together." I often wonder, if I hadn't had Richard, if it would have been easy – I don't know – to take the other children and say, "Put them in foster care, I just can't cope with them." But I wouldn't put Richard into foster care because I knew nobody would look after him and he'd be put in an institute and I didn't want that.

So he helped hold me together and I helped hold the other kids together. So we did it together. That's what I tried to explain to the parents. Some of them bought it and some didn't. But a lot of people can't understand why they have a retarded child. Even myself, I still find it hard. I think it's sad that people have to have children with something wrong with them.

I think it made me a better person. I think so. You often wonder what you'd be like if it didn't happen. But since it did, I hope I'm a better person for it. I try to be more understanding of other people. I try not to find fault with people. I try not to hold a grudge. I try to find good points in people – it doesn't always work, but I try.

Every Tuesday from one to two we have worship with the parents. We read different passages, discuss what they mean to us. We have a minister who is there to help. She gives her point of view but we also give our point of view. I would say our biggest disappointment was when we asked people what they thought heaven was like. Well, that was something else. I went home and said I would not go back to worship any more. I thought, when I left here, God was going to be there. If I lived a good life, he was going to pat me on the head and say, "Marlene, you were such a good little girl, now you are going to have everything you want up here." I always thought it would be nice to get married again and get somebody to share my life with. I was going to get up there and it would be just like living here. My grandmother passed away five years ago. She would meet me there but she would look like she did here. It was going to be a better life. I wouldn't have to work, but if I worked I wouldn't have to go through all the hard times – I figured I had that here. But at worship the other day people thought heaven wasn't going to be like here on earth. There would be something there, but they didn't think there would be human bodies. Oh, my goodness! "Well," I said, "you've got to be joking." I thought Richard would be there and he wouldn't be sick and lots of other people wouldn't be sick. I thought, I'm not going back there, they're just a bunch of loonies – they don't know what they're talking about. I really had to go home and think about that.

Then the minister couldn't do the service the next week and asked me would I do it and how could I say I wasn't going to? So I went, and we did the next passage that we had – of course we talked about heaven again because we were not leaving that high and dry. So we talked about it some more and it sort of sank in and it made a little bit more sense. I must say I am still disappointed. Then we talked about what we thought sin was and that was interesting, too. One woman said, "Well, if somebody murders someone, it's a sin." Somebody else said, "Yes, but if they have a problem, or if they are under pressure, they don't have enough food, whose fault is it, is it really their sin? Or the government's sin because we don't have enough to eat?" So we really got interested, but when you stop to think about it there's sins and there's sins – like, if you're stealing food because you need it. I don't know – I don't have the answer, either, but it really gets interesting and I really enjoy it.

You take the Bible from where it was supposed to be written and when it happened, and it revolves. The Bible's been fighting for rights for a long time, and it's sad that governments don't change. They change in a sense that it's not the same government, but the rich treat the poor the way they did all those years ago. The poor still have to beg. It's sad. It revolves.

When we went into Bible study we thought it was going to be such a pleasure, such an enjoyment. We thought we'd come out of there lifted or refreshed, and that doesn't happen to us. Because if we really get into the passage and put it into a context of what we learn and where we work in our community.... We work in a poor district – 75 percent of our people are on welfare or fixed incomes. I should say, maybe 55 percent are on welfare and the rest are on unemployment insurance. It's a poor district. If you take what we read and fit it where we think it fits in our district, it's sad. It's sad because people in general are good, I don't care what anybody says. You can tell me what you want, but I believe, down deep, people are good, born good, and circumstances turn things upside down. I hope I'll always believe that.

Our little church was Presbyterian – Baptist – United – Salvation Army – Pentecostal because we only had a little church and every week a different minister would come. We kind of got a whole mixture and we always got this image of Jesus as a man with a beard, and I guess I believed in that. I always believed that God was a man, but now I don't know. I think he's a very caring person; man, woman, whoever. I don't think he will ever do a miracle that will change the world. I believe, though, he gives people a push in the right direction. If we don't take it we lose it, and I don't think he gives you just one push. Somebody had to give me that push along the way – I didn't get all that strength by myself. I think God's there and he's caring and he tries to help everybody. Some react to that help, some pass it by. I think if I care for my children as much as I think I do, and they say God cares for you a hundred times more, then maybe I'm not alone. If God cares for me that much there is somebody who cares what I do and what I think and it helps me go. But I didn't get that just out of a book. It took me a long time to realize that, and maybe now that's what's holding me together. I'm not doing it by myself, for sure. I don't believe people can do it all by themselves because no matter what you do, you can do your job right at work, you can go home and do things right or whatever – the world's a hard place and you better be able to cope with things that are going to fall on you even if you don't want them to.

I don't see my husband very often. We're not enemies, we don't fight. I have never put him down. We both had our faults.

I guess I forgive my stepfather. I don't think you ever forget, but I don't go around holding a grudge. I guess he did what he thought he had to do to put food on the table. I guess he could have worked, but he didn't. I did hold a grudge for a long time, and I really don't want to do that. Maybe he did what he thought he had to do.

AS I LISTEN ⸻

As I listened to Marlene's story I was deeply impressed by the resilience of her spirit and by how far she had come in her pilgrimage. Her life began in poverty, a poverty she was to experience for many years in a variety of degrading forms. But there was worse than poverty. There was the fact that her stepfather was a bootlegger, and because of that she was shunned by the other children in the community, though she didn't know why. She was sexually abused from age 5 to age 13, a fact she mentioned almost in passing.

Her adult life was no better. Her husband abused her and finally abandoned her. A mentally handicapped child was born. Her mother said this was God's punishment for getting pregnant before she was married. Left alone with five children to support, Marlene clung to welfare as her only security.

But while she had been left a legacy of guilt and self-rejection, she was nevertheless able to respond – in fear and trembling – when jobs were offered.

This was a turning point in her life. She found that she did have something to offer. She found that she could participate in discussions about the Bible and about questions of faith. She was learning and growing. She found a few certainties in life, although other parts were still a mystery. She faced the future with hope, forgiving those who harmed her and grateful for what she received. What a pilgrimage! Marlene has achieved a remarkable degree of emotional and spiritual health.

AS I RESPOND

"It Took Me a Long Time to Realize it Wasn't True"

Many of us spend the first part of our lives learning one set of truths and the rest of our lives finding out that a lot of those truths are false. As I listened to Marlene I thought what a tremendous amount of baggage she had carried around. No wonder she had such a low image of herself. But Marlene is able to question others' truths, to get rid of that kind of baggage. It is a long process, but we can see it happening.

The first step is taken when she is abandoned by her husband and left with five young children to raise. It is a crucial moment. She hangs on somehow and ekes out a living on welfare, though she finds it demeaning. Then she is offered a job as a cook. She knows she can cook – it's about the only thing she knows she can do. But taking the job means going off welfare, removing the safety net. Can she risk it?

If what her husband told her is true, that she is good for nothing but staying at home and minding the kids and making sure his supper is ready when he decides to come home, then she should not take the job. She is not competent. Can she risk challenging his opinion of her? Can she support herself and the children by taking the job? It is a big risk. Marlene takes the risk. And, wonder of wonders, she is right and her husband was wrong! In a binge of celebration she buys all sorts of things she never had before.

The next test builds on the first. She has proved that she can hold a job. But that job was based on the one thing she knew she could do – cook. Now she has a chance to teach and counsel handicapped people. This job requires totally different skills. But people she trusts believe she can do it. That helps to challenge the low image she has of herself. Again, she takes a leap of faith.

Marlene doesn't stop there. She begins to ask questions like, Why is there injustice in the world? Why are children born handicapped? She no longer accepts the pat answers given by her mother and society. She is learning that things she was brought up to accept are no longer acceptable – are simply not true.

We can all identify with Marlene in this kind of discovery. I was not brought up in an atmosphere that deliberately diminished my self-confidence, as Marlene was. But when I look back, I can see how more subtle forces were at work that had a similar though less devastating effect. As the fourth of five children I lived in the shadow of my older brothers and sister. I seemed to be expected to follow in their footsteps – not to make any tracks of my own. Nobody said that, but that was what I felt. It was a time of economic depression, and our family income was low. Most of my clothes were hand-me-downs. I felt that most of my ideas were also hand-me-downs. Nothing new, nothing original.

Suddenly, at age 17, I went to university. I was on my own. It was frightening, but it was also exciting. I had to prove that I could choose my own courses and pass them. That wasn't too bad – I had done fairly well at school. Then, at the tender age of 18, I was sent for the summer months to a tiny rural community in northern Saskatchewan as a student minister. I was responsible for religious services in three localities, and for whatever pastoral care or other church responsibilities might be involved.

I think I survived more by my naiveté than by my ability. Nevertheless, I grew. I was called to do something that seemed far beyond my abilities. Perhaps that is where real faith starts. We are up against something that demands resources we don't have. In our desperation we dig deeper than we have ever dug before. And to our delight and surprise we discover a well within us we never knew existed.

Of course, the discovery is a gradual one, and it demands that we keep digging. Not all wells are artesian wells. It takes a lot of work to get down to the water, and still more to get it to the top of the well. But just knowing that the water is there is thrilling. Years later, Marlene realized that God had indeed been with her, giving her the strength she needed, the strength that "helped her go."

This faith in God is not a new kind of dependency. On the contrary, it is what brings out Marlene's faith in herself. She begins to see herself as a person with real potential. What has happened to Marlene is a kind of conversion. It is a conversion that comes from renouncing the image others have imposed on her and from believing in an entirely different image of herself.

It is a conversion that many of us need. We need to be converted from the low image somebody gave us, which we have accepted, to an image of ourselves as creations of worth and beauty. It is not an easy step to take, because the old image dies hard. The old image has a certain perverse attraction. We can say, "Since I have no gifts and have nothing to offer, I cannot be expected to become much. It would be foolish for me to accept much responsibility or to welcome a challenge. That would only be an invitation to failure." It is easier, in some ways, to remain on moral and spiritual welfare than to risk independence and responsibility.

Conversion involves repentance. Repentance, I realize, is not just being sorry for something I've done wrong. It's changing what I have let myself become. Strange, isn't it, that that comes so hard? Strange that I would sooner blame somebody or something else for who I am than embrace my real identity with joy? Strange that I would rather sweat and strain to prove to myself and others that I am not what I have seemed to be, instead of simply accepting God's gracious gift – "You are mine." It takes a long time, as Marlene says, to realize that what others say about us – and what we say about ourselves – *isn't* true. It also takes a long time to realize that what God says about us *is* true.

"It Revolves"

Marlene thought that Bible study would be something she could enjoy. It would be something new and interesting, a break from the harsh realities she lived with day by day. Alas, she was disillusioned. She became sadder, though wiser. Why? She is engaged in a struggle for justice – justice for people like the mentally handicapped and the poor in her district who seem condemned to their poverty. But in Bible study, she finds that people have been engaged in this struggle for centuries. Things don't change, they just revolve – they repeat themselves in some other form in some other place.

And God doesn't seem to do much about it. God does often show people the right way and give them a push in the right direction, as she says, but God doesn't step in and make the changes that so desperately need to be made. If things just revolve, why bother to try to do anything about them?

But Marlene doesn't give up in despair or cynicism. She doesn't understand why things revolve, but she does know that there have always been people, throughout history, who have kept on struggling. As she says: "The Bible's been struggling for rights for a long time." It's sad that things don't change, but the struggle nevertheless seems worth while. At least Marlene shows no signs of wanting to give up the work she is doing, or of becoming cynical about it.

I think Marlene is like Moses. He and his people dreamed of a Promised Land. They thought it would be a land "flowing with milk and honey." They spent a lifetime getting there. A whole generation died en route. Moses himself died, having only caught a glimpse of the land from afar. And when his people did get there it was never all they thought it would be. The Promised Land contained many enemies, and the battle against them seemed to go on forever. But the very vision of the Promised Land had in it the seeds of the vision of the kingdom of God, which so excited people like Jesus and many prophets and saints. The greatness of people like Moses is not diminished because they do not live to see their dream fulfilled. Perhaps Moses – and Marlene – help us to see that greatness and real satisfaction in life come not from arriving but from travelling toward what we believe in.

Perhaps they are saying, in effect, and quite unintentionally, that success is having a vision greater than anything we could accomplish in one lifetime, or in many lifetimes. Such visions don't condemn us to revolving with history, but they set up a creative tension between what is and what is meant to be. If there is any future for humanity on this planet, I'd like to share not only the hard realism but also the irrepressible hope that people like Marlene demonstrate every day of their lives.

"But I Didn't Get That Just Out of a Book"

One of the things that makes Marlene such an attractive person is that she doesn't think of her own well-being apart from the well-being of others, or of the world, for that matter. She learned that God was not going to heal her handicapped son by some big miracle. Nor is God going to heal the injustices of the world by some big miracle. She doesn't know why that is so, but it is so.

But other things are true, also. She doesn't think God is indifferent. "I think God's there and he's caring and he tries to help everybody. Some react to that help, some pass it by." So part of our troubles, and the troubles of the world, is not God's lack of caring but our lack of response.

But where does Marlene get this wisdom? Where did she find the caring God that helps her cope? She says, "I didn't get that just out of a book." People like Marlene are a healthy corrective for people like me who have been conditioned to believe that knowledge comes mostly from books, and from academic books, at that. Marlene has nothing against books – she is fascinated by the study of the world's greatest book, the Bible. But in the end, she is not dependent even on the Bible for what she knows to be true. She got a lot of garbled truths from different church leaders, and she got a real distortion of the person of God from her mother. But she put these to the test of her own demanding experience and she decided that God is a very caring person.

Reading in a book, the Bible, about humanity's long struggle against injustice broadened Marlene's understanding of the magnitude of the struggle, but it also confirmed what she already knew, from her own life, to be true. Marlene does not discount the importance of what I learn from books, but she does put book learning in its proper perspective. I should put my experience to the test of thorough studies made of the subject – and I should put thorough studies to the test of my experience.

Religion's final test is the test of faith. And faith like Marlene's comes only when it has been put to the test of our lives. In theological college I studied the arguments for the existence of God. But it was when I looked into the open graves of my wife and my daughter that I knew death was evil and powerful and God was loving and strong – and real.

I know that my experience, like Marlene's, is limited. Knowing something is true from my own experience does not mean I can force that truth on others. I must listen to their experience and learn from it. I know that what I have found to be true is not always a universal truth. But I know, too, that I must honour the truth I have found, and that I must test "universal" truth in my own life before it becomes real.

I remember taking a sermon of mine to a famed teacher of homiletics. He wrote at the bottom of it, "This may be true, but where are *you* in all this?" Apparently it sounded like something out of a book, not something I had proved in my own life.

I used to be reluctant to trust a truth or argue it on the basis of my own experience. I thought my life too small, my experience too limited. I still have some of that reluctance and in a way it may be a healthy reluctance. But not to put truth to the test in my own life, in real circumstances, is to reduce faith to mere opinion. And I have found, when some experience has been most intensely personal, it somehow, paradoxically, becomes most universal. That's how Marlene's experience affects me. What she has found to be true about God – that God is a caring God – rings true for me.

I don't intend to stop reading books – after all, many of them are truths distilled from others' experiences. But at the same time I am going to pay more attention to my own experience. Before I accept too easily what I read in some scholarly tome I will try to put it to the test in my life. I need to be sure, as Marlene says, that "it helps me go."

2

DON
The Struggle for Security

Don lives in a dingy room in a cheap hotel on the lower east side of Vancouver. He is about forty years old, unshaven, with long, straggly hair and ill-fitting glasses. He speaks with a hesitance that belies an underlying confidence.

I was adopted by my parents before I was 8 years old. Before that time it was different foster homes. I'd stay somewhere for a few months, then I'd move, and then I'd stay somewhere else, then I'd move. It became a way of life, which is probably still affecting me today. I still seem to be moving an awful lot.

These people were really good parents but I already had certain defenses and problems trusting people. It took me two or three years before I could accept that I was staying. These were learning years. A normal child, a child with a good home and family life is learning different kinds of things, like about the way things should be. I was thinking more about the situation, and that's a sort of adult thing, having to worry about the situation.

I can see what an enormous amount of patience it took for the parents to deal with this. I was thinking, "These are just people, they're going to be gone," and it took me a long time to realize they were in there for the show, for the duration, still are.

I guess I needed to be loved. I would go way out of my way. I used to be knocking on all my friends' doors at eight o'clock Saturday morning because I wanted to get out and be with my friends right away. Needed this love thing. And I'd be pestering the hell out of everybody, "Oh, no, here's this goddamned kid again," you know. I think I terrorized all my friends. I had this big need.

At school I had no concentration. I didn't care that much about it. How did I do in social things? Not very well, because I thought I was an outsider. I guess I thought I had something to prove that I was equal to everybody. So I did what any young guy'll do. I tried to be good at sports and I learned how to fight. And I was doing an awful lot of that.

I went to about Grade 9. About the age of fifteen I decided I should have my independence, grow up and get a job and leave home. So I did. I found out this was the adult world, and I didn't do too well in the adult world, let me tell you. I had a job for about three months in one of these factories. I don't know how I was getting paid, it seems very vague, but I can assure you it was the minimum. So I went up to the centre of the city, the hard core of the city, and I started hanging out. I disassociated myself from all other kids because I thought I had more experience – I got impatient with kids my own age. For a few years I lived on my own.

This was a tough period of my life. I wasn't working and I wasn't living at home. Of course there was no welfare, and this is the street-kid sort of thing, hanging around and having people take you in. I thought I was being an adult, taking care of myself and doing whatever I had to do to get a roof over my head. A little while later I landed up in jail. It just goes without saying.

I guess I was 18 the first time I went to jail, then 19. I did 18 months, and that was enough to turn me around. I got out, I was 21 and for some reason I had a turnover. Not that I decided to do anything. I didn't decide to make any great thing in my life or anything. I just decided that this wasn't the way it should be. I figured I'd get some schooling. I moved back home and I settled down and started thinking about things. I calmed down. I started doing a lot of things that were necessary.

For a year I lived at home. I think this was a rebuilding of myself, figuring out how it had been, what it really is. I had to go through this thing over and over again. I thought I should settle down and let the past be itself and think more about the future. Don't worry whether I'm good enough or whether I'm bad enough.

I couldn't really compare myself with people around me, and I didn't like comparing myself with myself. The early years were kind of crazy, and there wasn't any really high point in it so I had nothing to look back on and say, "Well, maybe I should go back to when I was like that because – every time I looked back it was worse. This was a survival thing. I shut myself off, not from people, 'cause I had this need for people, this love for people, but I shut myself off from myself, from my competitive side. I think that's the time when everything started to fall into place.

My relationships with women were really transient. I was always never quite in the door, never really out of it. I would be with different women. I think a lot of this reflects back to the orphan years. There wasn't a great deal of trust for women, which is too bad for me, I guess, 'cause I probably ruined a few relationships. And I was harsh on women – I had this need of lustiness and that.

And they didn't know how to have me there without me thinking that I always had to run out. So a lot of these women gave up. I would go off. By this time I was into drinking, and at one time I was doing a little dope. I was spending a lot of my time leaving. Some of the women I've known were really nice people and if I'd given them half a chance they'd have given me a lot more of a chance. I realize now they did give me a hell of a lot of leeway. They made very few demands. I seemed like a very transient person, and I don't know if this is good for women, but I think probably the truth is this is very bad for women.

It's one of the reasons I've sort of given up on relationships – I think it's bad for women, that a guy will move in but not really be there. Or only a part of him, and the other part will be – mentally anyway, and even physically – leaving, pulling away. That's how the relationships went.

I met this one woman when I was about twenty-one and until we were about twenty-four or twenty-five, we had a kind of relationship. It wasn't necessarily a sexual relationship. But we kept coming back to each other. Then something happened. I guess it just drizzled away; nothing came of it. The woman went off and got married. I was still transient at that time, thinking that nothing's permanent. I have this feeling that nothing's too permanent – including the church sometimes.

Around the age of thirty or thirty-one I had a series of relationships that were different. I started wanting to give people something. Maybe I wasn't capable of sharing myself with people but I wanted people to share themselves with me. I figured, well, if I can't find what I want I better see if I can do something for somebody else. I stopped talking so much and I started listening to people. I feel better about that time because I learned that one of the ways to share with people is to let them share with me. But when I start to share with people I still think, "Oh, I'm still in this transient state, I'm not far from getting on a bus and going somewhere." So it takes many years to become stable with people.

I'm afraid an awful lot of my life was – a job here, a job there, odd jobs. I was doing painting, unloading trucks, working in factories and warehouses. I worked for this lumber company. If I had decided at that time to make a career of anything, probably I could have done it. But I guess this thing's been plaguing me all my life. Well, I have to accept the fact that I'm ... sort of a transient person, I guess. If I did get a job I wonder whether I could work at it for 10 or 15 years. I'll be honest, it scares hell right out of me. To put 20 years into a job – I can't imagine that. I can't even see people being in that position. You know, the fear of it, being totally responsible for one's life is a – I guess it's a nice place to be but I think that's a hell of a thing. And to take a wife and raise children and decide to have a job – it would be a very traumatic thing, to say the least.

One of my friends was living the same life-style as me, and he decided to get a job and to leave the street life and build stability for himself. And he did. He started working at a 7-Eleven store. It's not much, right? But to us it seemed like a monstrous move. It takes a certain kind of values. Finding something in yourself. I think it's confidence and wanting to build a good life for yourself and for somebody else.

In my life I think this is a hell of a gap. I've been filling it with relationships and music. So this is probably the part when I started looking toward God.

I live right on the block here, a little hotel, it's quiet and it's nice. I love reading all kinds of stuff. An awful lot of fiction; a lot of what you call trash material; and a lot of other things, as well: theology books, psychology books, history books. All kinds of stuff. I read because I enjoy it. It's good. And I listen to people a lot. It really helps. I meet a lot of people through the Carnegie Centre (a community centre). I go there and do a lot of music. And through the church (First United Church) I meet an awful lot of people. I play guitar, piano, accordion. Picked it up by myself and started expressing myself musically. I've written a lot of songs. I'm writing about things I see around me. Feelings, emotions. And about relationships. A lot of the time it's not first person. I'll write songs about somebody else, or somebody else will talk to me and I'll write a song around someone else's experience or hopes or whatever. It's a way of expression. It's a release.

What keeps me going – besides food and cigarettes and beer? A lot of things. Depressed? Geez, no. I'm involved in a lot of things. Playing in places like The Smiling Buddha or The Classical Joint, hospitals, different drop-in centres. I do a lot of writing for the Carnegie newsletter. I was on the Carnegie Association

Board for awhile. I get involved with the church in a lot of different ways. I was really fortunate last year – I got a chance to do a sermon on a Sunday night. What really surprised me was they asked me in the first place. And I enjoyed it. It was a good experience.

Find the days long? Actually I wish they were longer. I wake up and they're too damn fast and I sometimes think, "Whoa!" The days are really quick, not like my life used to be when it was completely my own time and I didn't spend it too well. Oh, yeah, it's fast, it's fast. There are a lot of extremes. For a couple of weeks I was playing in The Smiling Buddha. It starts at 12:30 and goes to 2:30, 3:30 a.m. It's a pretty hard crowd. There's a lot of carousing around, drinking. Then the other extreme is I'd be coming into the church and working on different things, then I would be going to the Carnegie Centre, working with newsletters.

I'm fortunate that I've been able to do these things. I think everybody wants to contribute something to this damn life, not always take, take, take. I feel good about being able to give something back. I've taken my share. Prior to coming to this church I'd never had that much to do with church life. I'd just had my own beliefs. It's interesting to see how things come about and how decisions are made and how choices are taken.

Another surprise – I feel comfortable in this church. There's no stigma here, or if there is, people just keep it to themselves. So I just go about and be with everybody else and, you know, it feels good. Most Sundays I come down in the morning. I've got this porridge line going. About nine o'clock we make up a bunch of porridge; we put it out there in the front lobby and some of the guys come in. They don't have too much, like me, so they have some porridge – get started on the day. And it feels good.

I think I enjoy it when people do the sermons. For several years I believed in God and Jesus and all that, but when I was younger and used to go to church it would be very much centred around the word in the Book, and there wasn't much relationship with what's happening now to the Bible. But now I sit there and I listen and they seem to relate to what's happening today and they'll remember some story they read in the Bible as a child. It's not something that's too godly. I think it's the Christian faith, bringing Christianity to people in a different way. Not so much demanded of people. Not so much commitment, commitment, commitment. People are religious before they come to church or they wouldn't be there anyway. And I think the church has a better way of letting people express themselves without the church telling the people *how* to express themselves. People express themselves and the churches are trying to listen.

I think everybody's religious in one way or another. Between Christmas and New Year's there was an awful lot of violence on the streets; there were a lot of people injured, hurt. For some reason I had this feeling that it's a void in their lives. They're not expressing what they need to express, and there's only so many ways to do it. You can express yourself through religion or music, that's been my way all along. But people have to express themselves some way or there's this huge void. It leads to violence, frustration. In my life that was certainly the case.

It was like there was a big hole somewhere and I'd get drunk and that hole would be there and I would fight and I would express myself. Like I said, between Christmas and New Year's there seemed to be that hole I'm talking about – frustration, and no way of expression, so there was just incredible violence. And that's the time I think people subconsciously need to know there's a God, or need to know they're a part of the world and they have every bloody right to be here. And that's saying a lot when people are out there carousing around drinking and doping. Every now and then they got to get straight with themselves and say they have a right to be here – when really they don't feel that at all. They feel like they should be drifting and running, which is where I have come from. You feel you're not part of anything and you can't contribute anything, so you're drifting and running. You feel you have no place to be in God's world, and this is God's world. You have no reason to be any place for very long, because you have this built-in thing that says when people find out what a heel you really are ... you spend a lot of time running and moving.

So where to from here? I don't know. I was thinking, about three or four months from now, I'm going to try to get some money together. Not a lot of money – three or four hundred dollars. Me and a couple of my friends are going to go and do some recording. Make a demonstration tape, make about 30 copies, then go around and see if there's any kind of work I can manage to do. I'm not exactly what you'd call an image-seeking person. I'm not going into some high-class bar where they don't want music, they want a social performer. I'm definitely not a social performer. In the right place the music will be good enough, and the feelings can be good enough, and it won't matter that much, so that's what I'm going to try. It scares me, but it's what I can do fairly well, and I've done an awful lot of it.

It's just in the last year or two that people have been encouraging me. Before I came to Vancouver, this was in '80, '81, I was going through a booking agency in Manitoba and I played in small bars, all kinds of places, and we were making a bit of money. We'd play somewhere for a week, we'd get four or five hundred bucks. Then you knock off your expenses and bus fare. You'll still end up with a couple of hundred bucks clear. I was spending a lot, drinking a lot, but I was busy, doing things. I did it for a couple of years and I was on the go pretty good. I didn't actually manage to save anything, but I wouldn't say it was a waste because at least I was busy and it was sufficient and I was having a good life.

Whether I'll do it again, whether I can get it all together, get a house or apartment, I don't care, so long as day to day is good. That's fine with me. So I'll see where that leads, see what happens.

AS I LISTEN

Don's story of always being on the run, always fleeing from something or somebody, and yet longing to stay – to belong – reminded me of the story of Jacob, told in the Book of Genesis.

Jacob deceived his blind and aged father, Isaac, by passing himself off as his older brother, Esau, and so stealing his brother's birthright and blessing. Then, rather than face the consequences, he fled to his Uncle Laban. Once there, he took charge of his uncle's flocks and managed to end up, by clever deception, with the best of the herd. Again, when his deception was discovered, he fled – back home.

But then he had to face Esau, whom he had cheated. There was no place left to flee. The night before the dreaded meeting Jacob stayed on the banks of the River Jabbok, alone. Suddenly he was locked in a life-and-death struggle with a spirit that came up out of the river. "Tell me your name," demanded the spirit. In agony, Jacob cried: "My name is Jacob." It was the name he had been hiding all his life, and feared somebody would discover. "Your name shall no longer be Jacob, deceiver," replied the spirit, "but Israel, one who struggles with God." "Give me your blessing," begged Jacob. The spirit blessed him and departed.

Don was a kind of Jacob. He, too, dreaded coming face to face with his real self. Perhaps he felt he had been deceiving himself about his true identity, because he thought he could not acknowledge who he was and still keep his self-respect and the respect of others. Don was no cheater, but he struggled with his deep problem and ended up with a new self. Like Jacob, he was still far from perfect, but, like Jacob, he struggled with God and survived.

AS I RESPOND

"A Hell of a Gap"

Don's story makes me ask, "What are the blessings and curses of security? What is true security? Where do we find it?"

Don has been deprived of the sources of what we usually call security: a steady job, a solid relationship, family, a place to settle down, be it a house or an apartment. Don is caught between craving those things and fearing them. He says, "I guess it's a nice place to be but I think it's a hell of a thing." Mostly he is scared of security. "I'll be honest ... it scares hell right out of me ... being totally responsible for one's life."

I had asked Don what kinds of jobs he had held. It was a typical middle-class question – the kind of question we ask in order to get some sense of the history of a person, a history that is supposed to give us a clue to their character. Don's jobs have been odd jobs. He feels it would be odd for him to have a steady job. He tries to make it clear that he could have made a career out of a variety of things. It isn't that he lacks opportunity or ability. He chose not to have a steady job or make a career. It's something that has been plaguing him all his life. As he says, "I have to accept the fact that I'm a sort of transient person."

In the beginning it seemed he was transient because of circumstances. He never knew his own parents, and he went from foster home to foster home for the first eight years of his life. But he seems to be saying he is choosing to be a transient. He wonders if his decision is a cop out. He is angry that he is on the outside of the mainstream of life as most people think of it, and yet, damn it, he likes being a transient – or at least he *prefers* it. He knows his life is not perfect. He longs for confidence in himself and wants to build a good life for himself. He admits there is a hell of a gap in his life. He tries to fill the gap with relationships and music.

But Don's life isn't empty or boring, and it doesn't lack a sense of purpose or meaning. He doesn't have a house or an apartment, but he does have a base. He seems, on the whole, busy and content.

At first it may seem that I, and many people like me, have the kind of security Don lacks. I have a home, a job, definite responsibilities, lasting relationships. I don't sound like a transient. Yet, in some sense aren't we all transients? All looking for something we haven't yet found? All aware that something is missing, something important, vital, central?

I think of some of the people we think of as successful – people who have accomplished so much in their chosen profession and achieved wide recognition. Yet, upon closer examination, many of these people seem strangely like Don. They are running, running all the time, always striving for something that eludes them. On the way they may do a lot of good deeds or they may accumulate a lot of nice things, like a home and family and material possessions. They have a lot to be proud of, a lot in which to take satisfaction. And yet, at the end of the day, sometimes they feel, like Don, "a hell of a gap."

Some of them are workaholics, and what is working too hard but running after an ultimate goal? I've worked very hard in my day, as most full-time church workers do, and I called it dedication to God's work. Looking back, I think some of it was genuine dedication, but some of it was dangerously close to the rat race of many so-called secular jobs.

There are many pressures that make it difficult, if not impossible, to live a serene and balanced life. People who are perfectly free spirits may be irresponsible at times, unresponsive to great needs and duties around them. I am encouraged, when I read the Gospels, to find that Jesus often felt harried and stressed. Too many people were demanding too many things from him, and he could not simply pass them by. And yet his life did not seem out of control. I don't think we could describe him as a transient.

In a way he was like Don. Jesus had no home, no wife or children, no secure source of income. He said, "The foxes have holes and the birds of the air have their nests, but [I] have no place to rest [my] head." If there was to be security for him, it would not be found in home and family.

Where, then, did Jesus find security? When Don speaks about the hell of a gap that keeps bothering him, he says, "That is when I start looking toward God."

What has God got to do with filling the gap, with finding ultimate security? Can't religion be a form of escape, too? A kind of running from reality? It can, but it does not seem to have been for Jesus. When he felt the frantic pressures around him he took time to go off and pray. People sometimes chided him for that. Where have you been? they asked when he returned. Everybody has been asking for you. But Jesus does not apologize. It seems that he had to go off and pray in order to replenish his inner resources and also to establish his sense of direction. Where was all this frantic activity leading? What did it all add up to?

Jesus could hardly be called a transient. But perhaps we could call him a sojourner. Sojourners have only temporary homes, but they may well have a direction, a goal toward which they are travelling. In this way, Jesus was in the tradition of the Hebrew patriarchs, of the Hebrew people.

Abraham left the security and the gods of Babylon and went out "not knowing whither he went." But he did have a direction, a goal. He knew what he was looking for. As a later writer said of him, "He looked for a city which has foundations, whose builder and maker is God."

The Hebrews left a security of sorts, though it was the security of slavery, and went out into the wilderness. They wandered there for many years, but they did have a goal. It was the Promised Land. And they did feel that God was travelling with them, as evidenced by the pillar of cloud by day and the pillar of fire by night that went before them. That gave them a kind of security in their journey. They thought the place toward which they were heading was the right place, the place to which God was calling and directing them.

Jesus once said, "Take no thought for your life, what you shall eat or how you shall be clothed." Don seems to have heard and heeded that advice. But *somebody* has to care about putting food on the table and paying the rent. After all, Don couldn't do a lot of the things he does if our taxes didn't pay for his welfare. But Jesus is talking about priorities, about the ultimate direction of our lives. The second part of his advice is, "But seek first the kingdom of God and all these things shall be added to you." I hear Jesus saying to me, "Your job and your daily duties are important but put them in the perspective of your ultimate goal in life." When Don runs *from* a job and I run *to* my job, we may both be running away from the thing that matters most – the kingdom of God.

And what, pray, is the kingdom of God? I think Jesus is talking about something that is greater than any one of us and greater than any one of our lives. It is a universal, eternal goal, the direction in which all humankind should be travelling. Each of us has to translate that goal into something specific, which we see as a part of that greater whole.

25

Jesus said, "I have come, not to be served but to serve, and to give my life as a ransom for many." He warned us against lesser goals, goals that we could attain but that didn't lead to anything. He makes it clear that being part of the work of the kingdom of God did not have to be some spectacular, highly visible thing. Whoever gave someone a cup of cold water might well be doing the work of the kingdom, just as Don may be doing it on the Sunday-morning porridge line. But those who seek to serve themselves, Jesus said, are lost, while those who lose themselves in something greater than themselves in the end find their true selves.

Don says that when he feels the gap in his life, he turns his thoughts toward God, something, someone greater than himself, and yet something that helps him, and all of us, find true meaning and choose a direction in life. Therein lies true security.

"Every Bloody Right to be Here"

Don spoke about the violence on the streets between Christmas and New Year's. A lot of people were injured or hurt. Don tried to figure why this happened, and he concluded that it was because there was a big void in people's lives. What was the void?

Don seems to be saying two things, or perhaps they are two sides of the same thing. One is that people feel frustrated. For some reason they can't express themselves. So they fight, and their fighting expresses their frustration. The other thing Don is saying is that a lot of people feel they are not a part of anything, that they are nobodies, that they have nothing to contribute. That feeling leads to self-loathing or self-rejection. Some people want to run away, or just drift.

I can understand what Don means when he says that at Christmastime a lot of people feel keenly that they don't belong to anything. Other people are gathering in families or with friends and going to events sponsored by a church or other group to which they belong. People who don't belong to any groups feel left out. They feel they have nothing to offer and don't deserve to be included.

But I wonder if Don realizes that a great many people he thinks are included feel just as lonely and frustrated as he does? Does he know that many Christmas family gatherings intensify people's feelings of being different or alone? That even people in families feel like outsiders? Does he know how superficial many Christmas parties can be? How artificial the laughter and the camaraderie? Does he know that many people in cozy homes or well-appointed offices also may be feeling frustration? Does he know how many of them don't feel they belong, either? That they aren't a part of anything important? Is it not common to find people who feel they have failed completely and are left out of the mainstream of society because they deserve to be – that they just don't measure up?

I think Don's message is to stop trying to fight your way to self-acceptance. Stop running away from your feeling of no worth. This world doesn't belong to anybody, and nobody can decide whether you are of value or not. It's *God's* world, and it's God's gift to everybody in it. If it's a gift, you don't have to earn it or fight for it. Just accept it. Accept yourself because God accepts you.

That sounds to me a lot like the Christian doctrine of grace, the unmerited love of God. It reminds me of that wonderful verse: "It is by God's grace you are saved, through trusting God; it is not your own doing. It is God's gift, not a reward for work done. There is nothing for anyone to boast of. For we are God's handiwork" *(Ephesians 2:8-10)*. It's an elementary, fundamental thing, this gracious, unconditional love of God. But I know how often I forget it, or act as if it weren't true. I've done a lot of fighting in my life, and I've seen a lot of fighting. Call it violence, if you like. Only it's more sophisticated than Don's kind. It's called competition. Getting ahead. Reaching for the top. Free enterprise.

What if Don is right and all this striving is the result of a big hole in people's lives, a lack of self-acceptance? Are we fighting to prove ourselves, to put somebody else down, to trample over them on the way to the top? All the while, of course, there really is no top, no winning – only a constant fighting to avoid acknowledging that we are nobodies. All the while God says, You are somebody because I made you in my own image and I love you just because you are mine.

What if the whole armament race is the result of nations not feeling secure about themselves, feeling they have to prove they are number one by having the greatest arsenal of arms? What if the powerful gun lobby in the United States is the result of a big hole in people's hearts, so they feel constantly vulnerable and have to be ready to protect themselves by being able to kill somebody else?

After all these years, I have to be careful lest I spend my energies trying to

27

prove myself to others, or to myself, or to God. If I listened more to people like Don I might be able to begin with the belief that this is God's world and I have every bloody right to be here. Then I would be free to use my energy not to fight or run away, but to work with God in this world, which is both God's and mine.

3

DONNA
The Struggle to Change

Donna is 31 years old. She is of sturdy build, short hair, and pleasant face. She lives in a modest downtown apartment building in Toronto, with five cats. The apartment is bright and tastefully furnished. Donna speaks in a straightforward and direct manner.

I was born in St. Boniface, Manitoba, lived in the States for thirteen years, and two years in Australia. Wasn't too bad when we were younger. I think we were a pretty happy family, but I don't think any of us liked moving around a lot, and there were times when my father was gone for three months or six months because he didn't want the family to move again. I have three brothers and a sister. I'm in the middle. I think the longest time everybody was together was Louisiana, and I don't know what happened, but by that time everybody in the family was totally screwed up. All of us kids were into drinking and drugs, running away from home.

From the 7th grade on, until I quit, I was getting kicked out of school at least once a year, or I'd fail or get into fights. All my friends were getting into the same stuff. My parents had gotten really violent by that time and everybody was busy beating on everybody else. Not too good.

I think what happened between my mother and father was, she'd be left with all the discipline of the kids, and my father would go away and come back and spoil us rotten. So when my mother said on Monday, "You can't go out tonight, it's a school night," my father might come home that night and say, "Of course you can go out, do what you want. Here's some money, go party." Instead of taking it out on each other they took their anger out on their kids. I can't remember them just talking over their problems.

I think my mother resented not being able to go out and work because she couldn't leave us alone. Her mother died and she didn't make it to the funeral, which she blamed on us kids. I can see her point now. I certainly didn't see it then.

I was always different from the rest of the family. I hated people. I always loved animals. I can remember when I was two or three years old I liked people but my mother was always worried about me going up to strangers, sitting on their lap and talking to them. After I was five or six years old I couldn't be bothered playing with the other kids.

I finished 10th grade in New York. Then we moved to Louisiana again. When I got to Louisiana I needed another half credit to be in their 11th grade, and there was no way I was going to repeat 10th grade to get that half credit.

I was seventeen or eighteen. I did some baby-sitting for a friend, hung out, got stoned, went to jail, got out. A lot of time I was really screwed up. Sometimes I would steal my mother's car, go get some friends who lived in a group home, which they hated, and drive them out of the city. My little underground thing for runaways from group homes. It went on like that for at least a year after I quit school.

Then I came up to visit my brother in Medicine Hat for two or three months. When I got sick of it, I phoned to ask my father to arrange a plane ticket to go home. I'd left a dog behind that had just had a litter of puppies, I think it was eight puppies, and I called my sister and asked her how the dog was and she told me Mother had gotten rid of the dog, had her put to sleep with her puppies. I was extremely furious.

There was no way I would go back. I met this girl who had run away and we hitched to Toronto, where she thought her father lived. The first few days we camped outside police headquarters. We figured, we don't know the city, this seems like a safe place to be. They took us to Nellie's hostel. All I was doing was getting stoned a lot. After three days at Nellie's I got busted for theft and landed up in the Don jail for a little while.

That went on for many years. I wasn't doing anything. I got stoned on anything I could lay my hands on, acid, speed or whatever. Sometimes we would just shoot up whatever people had. We didn't bother asking what it was.

I think we got some money from mugging people, which didn't last too long, because the friends I was with insisted on mugging elderly people, which was totally against anything I believed in. Some of us would share a room. Whoever could get on welfare would pay the rent, and the rest of us would go out and steal food. We ate real good back then because we'd steal steaks and cheese and whole wheat bread, and somebody would go steal cigarettes. We never got caught.

I can't remember the first permanent place I lived in. Probably with my friend Beth. I met her when I was living at Nellie's. She told me I could live in her house for awhile until I made up my mind what I wanted to do. I lived there for about a year. That was probably the first place in Toronto I considered home. Can't remember what year it was. By the time I came here I hated my family, but then I also wanted a very healthy, normal, together, loving family that would stick up for each other. My parents still don't consider that they were violent or any of us in the family were violent.

And yet, I remember once, when we lived in Louisiana, my mother told me this story. She told me, I was really pissed off at my older brother and I was chasing him with a pitchfork, and if I had caught him, that pitchfork would have been driven right through his guts. My mother said, "I should have known there were problems when I felt I had to sit on the back patio with Dad's .22, knowing that if you caught up with your brother I'd have to shoot you." "Mum," I said, "didn't that tell you something was wrong somewhere? No violence? No violence at all?" She never told me that story before so I really don't know if it happened. I don't remember because I'd get so angry I wouldn't notice that the rest of the world even existed. Even if that was just how my mother felt about things, she should have kind of clued in to it. She's a funny lady.

Then Beth kicked me out. I was still doing drugs, and I was on medication from the shrink, and any time I'd get a prescription I would just take the whole bottle and try to do myself in. So finally Beth felt, well, I can't handle any more in my house. I was in the hospital and she came and told me she couldn't handle any more, and that was fine with me.

One of the nicest things about Beth is that when she came to tell me I couldn't move back into her house, she also told me to keep the keys. She said, "You're welcome any time, day or night, you don't have to call, you don't have to let me know you need to be here. Just walk in." So it was kind of like being kicked out but it really wasn't.

Me and a friend, Susan, we were best buddies. We spent all day together, did things together. We were getting fed up and we decided to go out west to visit my parents. So we drove out there in her car. My parents had assured me that I could go to Montana for Christmas and nobody would be drinking or fighting.

We left her car in Medicine Hat and went to Montana in my parents' car. Right from day one people were getting drunk and were fighting. So I told her, we're going to leave, that's all. And she said okay. I knew my father had this handgun I really liked, and he always kept it in his desk. I knew where he kept his keys so I got them and took his handgun and all the bullets. I thought, while I was at it, I might as well take all his rifles. We threw our clothes together and got in the car. I told my parents, "We've had enough, we're leaving."

Well, they checked and found that everything was gone and they called the cops. We were barely out of Alberta when the RCMP stopped us. There were like about 20 cars. They all jumped out of their cars, they pointed their rifles at us and said, "Come out with your hands up." That was it for me. I could not stop laughing. I just couldn't stop. They took us to Swift Current, and we spent the night in jail there. We went to Medicine Hat. They had us in the forensic unit for awhile. They thought maybe we were a bit nuts. Then we went to jail in Calgary, and then a couple of months at Fort Saskatchewan jail. Then we came home. I don't think I was ever in trouble with the law after that.

I've been celibate now for about 10 years and I've decided not to worry about relationships, about dating, and can this guy be trusted and what is he going to do. I can go out with guys I know and have a good time, and they know exactly where I stand. It's certainly opened up a lot of trust between me and guys to just be friends and trust them.

When I was a little kid I usually got along better with the boys in the neighborhood. But when I was 12, I was raped by my older brother. That was after my father got violent. I tried talking to my parents. I said, "You know, Bob's bothering me, can you get him away from me?" They said I was crazy; I was imagining things. They made it perfectly clear that I was just a sick girl and that I shouldn't talk about my older brother that way.

When that happened, I wouldn't talk to anybody. My older brother got more violent, then my father got more violent. My friends' fathers got more violent. At that time I thought, I can't deal with this shit. By the time I came to Toronto I didn't trust guys at all, except as friends.

Sometimes I miss not being able to get my shit together enough to settle down and have a family. I don't think I'll ever get into a relationship. But I think women, when they get into their thirties, start really longing to have a family. I have friends that aren't in relationships, either, and don't want to be. Some of them are gay, but there's still that longing to bring life into the world. But then I start thinking that maybe one day, after I have not been in trouble with the law for a long time and have worked for a while, I hope I'll be able to convince the Children's Aid Society I would be a good mother and be able to adopt a handicapped child. That is what I'd really like to do. But the CAS is always saying that certain people will never be able to adopt a child – "we have to protect the children." It pisses me off because they have all this stuff in the newspaper about foster families and not enough people around that want kids.

I've got a pretty good support system that consists of people who have known me since I've been in Toronto and have never turned their backs on me, who are always there, whether I was in jail, in a hostel, on the streets, being mouthy. I guess they saw something in me I didn't see in myself, because for a long time I didn't think I'd ever be where I am today. I never thought I'd be able to hold down a job. I never thought I'd live past 30. I tell you, my 30th birthday party was a hell of a celebration.

I think the big turning point for me was after that incident in Medicine Hat. Me and Susan had an argument one morning. She said "Good morning," and I said, "Don't talk to me, I'm in a bad mood." I don't know where the hell her head was at but she got in the car and went home and overdosed and died in the hospital later that day. It was one death too many. And I think that was a big thing for me. I've known other people who have died – either they were murdered or did themselves in or took an accidental overdose. I'd had good friends but I'd never had a best buddy. We thought a lot alike, and our experiences were similar. We wanted the same things in life, so she was my best buddy.

I guess I went into shock and when I came around I was in Queen Street psychiatric hospital. After a while I got out and I lived in a room in a rooming house. I thought there's got to be something else. I'd just had enough. Something just clicked. Nothing was perfect after that.

My cats were boarding at the Endangered Animal Sanctuary. I realized it wasn't fair to them, because they were kept in a cage most of the time. I got them out. After I got the cats out I started pulling it together. My parents always used to have my animals put to sleep when they got tired of them, and it occurred to me that they were my responsibility. One of the cats was Susan's, and that kind of helped in a weird way. I thought, If I don't give a shit if she died – to hell with her, I'll take care of her cat.

I decided that things had to be different, but I had no idea what needed to be different. I went to school on and off for a couple of years, which was good, because it gave me something to do with my time. It allowed me to start feeling a little better about myself, and it was kind of fun. I met some new friends. I started trusting people. My friends have helped. They trusted me. Beth always had me baby-sitting her daughter when other people were warning her, "What the hell are you letting her take care of your house and kid for?" But she trusted me. I guess there were a lot of things that helped turn me around.

Now I'm working in a group home. Residential counsellor is the official title. There's seven of us who work there. It's a collective and we run the house. It's a government group home set up to help people who have been through the psychiatric system, a place where women can come and be safe, feel safe. We don't tell women, "You've got to get your shit together and you've got to do this, this and this, otherwise you'll get kicked out." We help them figure out what they want to do with their lives. A woman might come in and say, "I don't want to hurt myself anymore, so while I'm living here I will not hurt myself, and my future goal is to get a place that I can afford to live in and keep healthy." We try to help these women take control of their lives. Whatever they decide to do is fine with us, because it's their life. Pretty simple stuff.

I don't think of this work in terms of what I've got to give the women living there. It was always a dream of mine to work as a veterinarian. Then I realized I didn't have the brains to do that kind of scientific work. The only thing I could come up with was that I'd like to work with people. I can't say I have anything different to give the women at the group home. I don't treat them any differently than I treat my friends. If I get pissed off, they know I'm pissed off. If I'm in a good mood, they know I'm in a good mood. There's no secrets. They know exactly what I've been through in my life, because they ask questions and I answer them.

I can't draw a line between the people living there and me. There are two women there I knew before. I was with one of them in Queen Street psychiatric hospital, and I was with the other in hostels. How could I treat them differently? I *know* them! I guess the thing I like about the job is that I don't have to act. It's a job where I can be myself.

I think I feel pretty good about myself. I'm doing okay. I even got an RRSP this week. I got the apartment insured last week. Middle-class things I didn't think I'd get into. The longer I'm off the street, the more worried I get that I'll become one of those people who get their lives together, then put other people down. I'd fight like hell to prevent that from happening. One friend I met here at the hostel the first year I came to Toronto. She's one of the people who just kept in touch, never turned her back. She always says, as long as you're worried about it happening, it will never happen. So I guess I'll have to keep my act together and keep on worrying – at least an hour a day to worry in, so I don't become too uppity.

I think I could be doing more with my life. There is this vigilante group – it's the only name I can think of for it – in Cabbagetown. These people have moved from the suburbs and bought the rooming houses – you know the type. They are anti-prostitution. They want the hookers to work on Bay Street. They are determined they are going to get the hookers off Ontario and Dundas Streets. This is their neighborhood now. They really piss me off. It's not that I believe in prostitution or don't believe in prostitution. People do what they have to do with their lives. But telling people to get out of the neighborhood because it's not their neighborhood any more is not the way to go about things.

The streets belong to everybody. If you don't like walking out of your house and seeing condoms on the ground, it's too damn bad. If anything, the street belongs to the people who have no choice but to live there. People from the suburbs can get drunk and puke all over the street and go home to a nice warm bed and somebody will look after them and wipe their brow. But there are people sleeping on those sidewalks they're puking on. I think everybody has a *right* to a home and I don't think these people have a right to move in and put people down that have lived here a long time. Sad bunch of people. I wouldn't trade places with any of them for anything. I have no idea what makes them that way.

I'd like my job to stay as good as it is, and I'd like to have just one job for the rest of my life. I would like to adopt a kid. I don't have any really grand dreams for myself. I don't want to be famous. I'd like my life to be quiet, to be able to do what I feel I have to do, want to do. I like it simple. Sometimes I like having money to buy new things. I definitely like having money to spend on people, which is lots of fun. I'd like to travel a bit around Canada. I don't want too much.

AS I LISTEN

Donna was born into a middle-class family but she rejected middle-class standards and life-style. She rebelled. It took her a long time to develop an alternative way of life, with her own standards and values. In a sense, she marginalized herself.

A life of almost complete self-indulgence did not satisfy her in the long run. She could not go on, but she could not return to what she had rejected. She had to find something new and different for herself. She used her experience in a creative way, and shaped it to her newly defined values and aspirations.

Her life is a journey. It is one example of the amazing resources of the human spirit. No wonder she celebrated her 30th birthday!

AS I RESPOND

"She Told Me to Keep the Keys to Her House"

Donna's experience of home is so different from mine that it challenges me to define what I mean by the word "home." Donna was deprived of a real home – the kind many people dream of, and which some of us are given. She says, "I hated my family, but then I also wanted a very healthy, normal, together, loving family that would stick up for each other." She never got it. But to her surprise and delight she found someone who became a family, who provided a home. And she made friends.

There was Susan, her best buddy, whose death was a tragedy. There are the women with whom she works, people who need her and to whom she gives herself freely. They are her family, and she feels at home with them.

All this says to me that my concept of home needs to be greatly enlarged. Donna's disappointment with her home, and her alienation from it, forced her to seek out or create a home of her own. I see how fortunate I was to have parents who loved me, and sisters and brothers who formed a secure community for me, and how blessed I was with people who took over where my family left off. Not that my family ever left me, but circumstances created a certain distance. This was inevitable. We moved to different parts of the country, thousands of miles apart. We married and formed our own families. We entered different vocations. We developed different interests.

It is one thing to long for and work for a home where we will always be welcome. It is another thing to think of that home as a place where we never have to grow up. When I try to follow this truth to its origin, I come to the Garden of Eden. That was humanity's first home, a place created especially for Adam and Eve. But there were conditions for living there. If people wrote their own rules, the intention and character of the garden would be destroyed. And, in a sense, the people would be destroyed, too, and they would not be able to fulfill their true humanity. When Adam and Eve ignored the rules and indulged themselves in a way that could be fatal for their future, God evicted them. That was the only way they could be helped to act responsibly, to be what they were intended to be – people made in the image of God.

That's what Donna's friend Beth was doing when she told Donna she couldn't stay with her any longer. Donna had been using Beth's home to avoid making responsible decisions. She violated the terms of Beth's invitation. So Donna was kicked out – but not really. Beth told her to keep the keys.

That, I think, is what God does. Adam and Eve have to leave the garden, but God never abandons them. God is with them as they make a new life and establish their family. In a way, the rest of the Bible is a series of stories of how people get kicked out and come back, because they always have the keys when they need them. In the process they grow up and become responsible for their own actions, and they help to maintain a home and provide a place for others.

As I think about Donna and Beth and home and God, I realize that there are some people who never find a friend like Beth. There are times when many of us feel that for some reason our Beth has died or disappeared, times when no one – not even God – seems to be home when we go there in a time of desperate need.

I think of Jesus on the Cross, when all his friends had run away and when even God seemed absent. He cried the most desperate of all cries: "My God, my God, why hast thou forsaken me?" And there was no answer. Has God locked the door and taken the keys? Have we lost the keys or forgotten the address? Why wouldn't God come looking for us? Are there times when we are abandoned – left completely homeless?

Nobody seems to have found an answer to that question. Yet when Jesus felt most godforsaken, it was to God that he cried. This is a mystery that many saints and seers have experienced and wrestled with. It can lead to deep bitterness or deep holiness.

Donna hasn't yet felt totally forsaken. She has grown immensely. By opening herself to the disturbed and needy women in the place where she works, she is providing a home for them.

All of which makes me think that my search for a true home as a refuge in time of need is only half the search. The other half is something that challenges me, and frightens and excites me. It is the searching for – no, the growing to become – the kind of person who is used by God to be a Beth to others.

Otherwise, how will people know there is a love that never stops loving, and keys that are never taken back?

"Something just Clicked. Nothing was Perfect After That"

This is a moment of dramatic change. A transformation. Christians might call it a conversion. Here was a person who had done her best to destroy herself with drugs and had rejected everyone's efforts to help her. A parasite on society, some think. She had little or no self-respect. There seemed nothing to work with, nothing to build on.

Then, her best friend – her only really close friend – takes her own life, it seems, because of a silly remark Donna makes. "Something just clicked. Nothing seemed right after that."

This is indeed a conversion. Except that there is no mention of God in it. No mention of Christ, Bible or church (except negatively, for the most part). Are those things peripheral or irrelevant?

That would certainly not be true for me. Those things informed me, challenged me, inspired me, sustained me. But what I am sensing in Donna is something that is not contradictory to those great words and traditions. Rather, it illuminates them.

Let us think of some great words for a moment. Take the word "God." The great theologian, Paul Tillich, talks about "the God above God." There is, in other words, more to God than "God" – more than any word or concept humans can describe. So the word "God" always points beyond it to something greater. Yet God must be given some characteristics or God ceases to exist or to have any meaning. We all have to decide upon some of these characteristics, knowing that they must all be open to rejection or revision or addition as we come to understand God more fully.

Everyone who speaks of God has some characteristics in mind. But any belief in God is ultimately related to or defined by the way we act and the decisions we make. Our actions and decisions reveal our true values, the standards we live by. These standards evolve out of watching other people's standards and choosing to accept, modify or reject them.

Donna grew up in a very confusing and violent environment. She rebelled against the standards of her family and spent a long time in the wilderness, indulging herself, acting with no direction. Then she met Beth. Beth was a model. In a way, Beth became a God figure – someone who loves unconditionally, yet has definite criteria by which to judge behavior. When Susan took her own life – an act of ultimate violence – Donna had a choice to make. Perhaps she saw, in Susan's death, a picture of herself. Perhaps she saw that, rather than renouncing her family's violence, she had perpetuated it. She could take her own life, as she had often attempted before, or she could renounce violence and choose love. She chose love. She renounced her mother's violent model. She took Susan's cat home and took care of it.

I believe that this choice was Donna's way of professing a belief in a God of love. She had a choice between a God who was a destroyer, a God of violence, or a God who was a savior, a God of love. Her subsequent actions and attitudes indicate the choice she made. Compassion is high on Donna's list of virtues. It is a virtue she finds sadly lacking in many people. People who make compassion a standard cannot be far from expressing a belief in a God of love and caring. They might not use the word "God," nor should we insist that they do. It is the *character* of God we are talking about here, not the name.

There are definite biblical overtones in Donna's story. To be sure, she does not mention the Bible. The Bible is a variety of things, but for many it is a record of people's search for God and God's search for people. The stories in the Bible have been preserved because people find in them something with which they can identify, a help in their search.

When Susan died, Donna came to the end of her tether. She suddenly came to herself. In a way, she came "home" to Beth after her years of wandering. Could this not be a story of the Prodigal Daughter? A very biblical tale?

Donna was not influenced by the Bible in her momentous decision. But what we who know and love the Bible can say is that Donna's story is a continuation of the Bible story, or a parallel story.

If we ask where the church comes in, we have to admit that the church had some negative connotations for Donna. She was turned off by people who go to church but who act selfishly. But the church cannot be limited to a certain institution, any more than God can be limited to one concept. The church is a fellowship of people who hold certain beliefs and who band together to share and promote those beliefs, to care for one another, and to join in caring for society and the world. In this sense, Donna does belong to a church. She has a support group of people whose beliefs she shares and who care for her. In turn, Donna cares for them and for others outside the group and for the society in which she lives.

But in a very real way, Donna also belongs to the church. Christians say there is the visible church, but also an "invisible church." The invisible church, like God, always transcends anything humans can fully comprehend, and includes many more people than any institution or definition could include. I believe Donna belongs to that church.

"Christ" is the name people gave Jesus when they saw him as an agent and expression of God's love. In giving him that name they became his followers. Can we not say that, in devoting so much of her life to working with ex-psychiatric women, and in working for what she feels is justice for street people, Donna has heard a call to love, and has followed it? Is it not a Christ-like thing she is doing?

It would be hard to imagine Jesus rejecting a person like Donna, or requiring her to conform to certain prescribed patterns. He would, I believe, recognize in her a genuinely spiritual person. We remember how, according to the Gospel of John, in speaking with a woman in Samaria, Jesus refused to become involved in the argument about whether God should be worshipped on a Samaritan mountain or in the temple in Jerusalem. God is spirit, said Jesus, and those who worship God must worship in spirit and in truth. That's what Donna does. I think she has caught the spirit of Christ.

Donna does not need Christians to legitimize her conversion. It is there for all to see and celebrate, and they do not need to use the word "conversion" if that is not their kind of language. But neither does Donna's conversion invalidate the sources and criteria Christians find helpful. What is helpful for me, as a Christian, is to reflect on Donna's conversion and to see how it illuminates some of the words Christians use.

Words and concepts, religious or secular, that have been in use for a long time, need periodically to be rediscovered and redefined. Don helped me to redefine the word "security." Marlene helped to redefine the word "repentance." Donna helps us consider the concepts of "God," "Bible," "Church," and "Christ." She helps us look at the meaning of "conversion." She helps us to think of the spirit, rather than the letter of these words.

We remember that marvellous statement attributed to Jesus when he was talking with Nicodemus. Nicodemus was a learned, righteous man. But he could think only in terms of well-established forms. Jesus told him he had to be "born again" – born of the spirit, freed to see God wherever God appeared. He should not try to keep God in a box. "The spirit blows where it wills," said Jesus, "and you cannot tell where it came from or where it is going. So is everyone who is born from spirit."

I think Donna was born from spirit. I don't have to ask, "But where did that spirit come from?" Or, "Where is it taking her?" Thank God I can't control the source and destination of the spirit. Donna helps me to celebrate it wherever and whenever I see it.

4

LORNE
The Struggle for Self-Acceptance

Lorne is a Native Canadian in his early fifties. He is a large man with black hair and a square face. There are deep creases in his face that have the effect of making it look almost like a sketch drawn with bold strokes of a brush, or like a sculpture chiselled out of stone. He speaks softly, almost shyly, but with little hesitation. Occasionally he chuckles at himself, revealing a becoming modesty and sense of security. He lives in a tiny apartment in a low-cost housing building erected by a church in downtown Toronto. The room is sparsely but adequately furnished. There are no signs of native art or artifacts, except for a single feather stuck in a wall clock. Lorne has served as a counsellor with alcoholics and drug addicts. He is now on disability pension because of chronic trouble with his legs.

I was born and raised on a little reservation between Sault Ste. Marie and Blind River on the north shore of Lake Huron. About 12 years of my life were spent on that reservation.

It was during Depression time and I can remember them building a highway through there and my dad worked on the relief gang – they were giving, I believe, 10 cents a day. I had never seen a steam roller or a steam shovel in my life and I can remember the first steam roller comin' down the road and I got horribly afraid of it.

It wasn't easy livin' on the reservation. You were governed by the mounted police and they used to always go by the house to make sure you didn't catch too many fish. My dad was a good spear fisherman and I used to go with him down to the falls and we'd catch these sturgeon. He'd spear them and I'd watch him and he showed me how to do it and we would come home and we would smoke them for the summer.

We always had enough food, even though it was Depression time. It wasn't much – it was mostly fish and wild potatoes and a few hazelnuts. They were easy to come by at that time.

My dad worked in the sawmill so we moved down near Blind River. But they wouldn't let me go to town. I used to see the other kids playing ball on the field across from where we lived. I used to sit up on the rocks and watch them. They seemed to be having a lot of fun. I used to question my parents about if I could go to school because I always wanted to be an aviation pilot. And they always said I would go to school in time, but I was getting pretty old – I was 8 years old.

There were five other children ahead of me. I was the last one. I can remember asking them to send me to residential school if they couldn't afford to send me to the school in the town, and they said no, they didn't want to send me to residential school.

However, I forgot about school and I started to learn how to cut wood and how to fish and started harmonizing with nature. My mother and father drank a lot and I guess they don't know the mental torture they put me through when they used to go to town and wouldn't come back for hours. And I knew at a certain time if they weren't back that they were drinking. I used to sit by the window and I'd watch and I'd watch and I'd watch. I was afraid that they might drown coming across the river. It never happened, but I was always worried about it.

I finally went to school for a year when I was about eleven years old. I went to a public school in Blind River and I guess I was the biggest kid in Grade 1. I'm pretty fast, and even though I only went one year they moved me from Grade 1 to Grade 3 and I was going into 4. The year after that my father was a foreman at a lumber camp, and I came home after school one day before Christmas and my mother told me that my father wanted me to quit school. I was supposed to go to work.

During the time I went to school I had a lot of fights. I even fought with the principal toward the end because I was always fighting. But I was only trying to protect myself from kids that were picking on me. But they were smarter than I – they always got away before the principal come along, and I was the one that was caught. So I rebelled. I was glad to get out of school.

In January of that year I went to work. I was 12 years old. I didn't know what to expect. I started to work in the kitchen. I'm grateful to the people I worked with at that place – they taught me a lot about hygiene, how to dress, what clothes to buy, and they told me a lot of what life was all about. But of course I learned the bad habits, too. I learned how to smoke, how to curse and swear.

I stayed there for three months. We used to feed about 350 men in the morning and at night. There was a hot lunch delivered to them. We used to get up at four o'clock in the morning and start preparing breakfast, and we wouldn't get to bed till ten o'clock at night, and we had all those dishes to wash!

When I was 13 years old I took a man's job and they put me cutting logs. Another man and I used to have to cut 120 logs a day with a crosscut saw. By the end of six months I knew what to do. The following year I could do it myself. I learned how to roll logs, to drive horses – I could do any job in the sawmill. I was 14 years old.

The next year I went back as a sawyer. I loved the speed of it and I loved the action. You couldn't stop – you never had time to think of anything – when the carriage carrying the logs goes, it's like a blur. It was always a steady go, steady go, steady drive, drive, drive and that was an eight hour day. I loved it.

I taught myself how to do math. I used to go home at night and I'd sit there and I learned how to do fractions and how to add and multiply. But I got away from that. I guess I wanted to get out and see more of what the world was about. So I did.

But I didn't go very far. I went as far as Sault Ste. Marie, and I didn't learn too much, either. I was about fifteen then. I worked in the pulp-and-paper mill there for awhile but the city didn't seem right to me – it was too much, too fast. There was no rest. Even if you stayed in the rooming house there was people coming and going all the time. It didn't agree with me, so I went back to work at the lumber camp for awhile. Then I went to the mine. I was healthy, I weighed l80 pounds and I didn't have any trouble getting into the mine. I was making not too bad money. I stayed for about a year, I guess. But I got tired of working underground. I couldn't breathe properly. After about eight months I found that I was coughing steady so I got out of there and went somewheres else.

I got married when I was 17 years old. I figured I was starting to wander too much, so I thought maybe I'll settle down if I got married, which I did. I married a Scotchwoman from Massey, Ontario, and I don't think I married that woman because I loved her. I hated being a native person, and I knew how the native people were getting treated, and what they were saying about them. So I got this bright idea that I was not going to be a native person and I married a Scotchwoman. I wanted to be better than a native person.

I think that marriage lasted about seven years. The first five, six years was good, but then it started to go on the rocks and I found something else – I found alcohol. I didn't drink that much, but I drank.

We didn't have any children and I think that was the worst part of it. That hurted her. I guess I was running myself down, too: "Well, I'm not good enough – I can't make babies...." I guess the word is "inferior." But I used to go to work, I drank, I'd come home drunk, and she got fed up with it. She told me: "It's either gonna be me or the bottle. Which is it?" I preferred the bottle. She says: "That's fine." We separated, we went our different directions.

I came back about seven or eight months later. I was coming back to make amends to my wife. I got off the bus and the police were there waiting for me with a non-support charge. I spent the night in the police station and the next morning I went to court. The judge read the charge against me, called my wife up. I never said anything to her, just let her say what she wanted to say. He said, "You got anything to say for yourself?" I said, "No, I haven't" – I didn't want to fight. And he said, "I want you to pay $150 a month for support. The $150 is for the child that's coming." I blew up! I just literally blew up when he said that. And I said, "Why should I have to pay for somebody else's child?" I couldn't understand this. I blew up, and the police held me down, and I finally settled down and the judge said, "You can leave now."

So I went out and the charge stood.

I walked out and went to the Hydro office, where I had worked and where I knew I had some cheques coming. I got them and I left and I never bothered paying what the judge ordered. I was still so angry. I went to the States. I worked there for awhile but I couldn't quite get along and I started drinking more and more. I came back to Canada and worked in the mines, then in a sawmill, where I was supervisor for 12 years. I could have made it there – making good money, didn't drink for awhile. But I gave up again. I couldn't settle.

In the meantime, my wife had about five children and laid two more non-support charges. The last one, the magistrate threw it out. So that was that. So what I done was ... I decided to make an amend.

I went to work in Garson mine. I bought a house there. After I got everything set up I told her she could move in with the kids. I fixed up the basement and rented it as an apartment for $400 a month, and all that money I put away as long as I was working and staying there. I had my room in another part of the house.

I was trying to save as much as I could for the kids so they could get an education. Even though they weren't mine. I went to see a lawyer and asked him if he would make sure that house couldn't be sold by nobody, not even by me. It took me 12 years to do all this and when I thought I had enough money saved up for those kids to go through university I went and saw the lawyer and told him how much money to give each child, but only for the university, nothing else. Then I packed up one morning, put my clothes in the trunk of an old car I had, and I left. I never went back.

I went up to Timmins, worked around there for awhile, and that's where I got into the restaurant business. Then I got into a restaurant, gas station and motel business on Chapleau Highway – Good Lord! The money I blew there! Another drinking spree. Finally I came to the big city, Toronto, looking for the gold they were talking about in the streets. But I made a mistake. I had a job for a few years here, a fairly good job, and I started drinking. Y'know, I wrote a poem called "Stations." It describes what life to me was about: I went through life like I was going through on a train.

I went back up north and I really sunk down. I knew I was getting on in age – I was about forty then – and I needed to have faith. I never had no spiritual links with the Indian people, other than different stories they told me. I didn't quite understand what it was all about.

But once, I was in jail for a drunk charge and I had a bad leg – it was swollen right up – and they took me to the hospital. The doctor said I had a fever of 105 degrees. They laid me down on the hospital bed and I said, "Oh, God, don't let me die!"

I thought I was asleep, but as I was laying there a picture appeared in front of me, a picture of Christ, brown hair, a brown beard, and a scarlet cape, and he had his hand up in the air. And when his hand moved to the right everything seemed to go out of me – everything just left me. The pain in my leg and the fever just seemed to go. I thought I was dying.

The doctor and the nurse came in and examined me and the doctor said, "What happened?" I said, "You know, if I told you, you wouldn't believe me." I went back into myself and I felt normal, I felt good. And I wanted to find out what it was. I asked to see the priest and I talked to him. He told me it was an optical illusion. But how could an optical illusion make you feel perfect? I was a little bit afraid. I thought, Something's gonna happen to me – something horrible.

After that I started drinking again. A year later, something happened to me. I was in a hospital bed and they had given up on me. All of a sudden, I'm by the window. But I can see my body laying in the bed, and I'm saying to myself, "Now how did I get here?" I could see the traffic going by outside, but I couldn't see myself. The nurse come in, she looked at me and she ran out. I was screaming at the top of my voice, "I'm over here!" The nurse couldn't hear me – she was gone. Then I could hear her and the doctor running down the hallway. And I thought, Now, how am I gonna get back into my body?

The doctor took the stethoscope, then looked at the nurse. He said, "You're sure?" She said, "I'm positive." That's all I heard. I was able to eat that night, and the next day they put me on full diet. A week later I was released from the hospital.

But I got scared. I was really frightened. I started drinking more and more. I really wanted to find something spiritual.

So I started to go to church, and every time I went to a church I would get filled up with something inside of me and the tears would just about burst. But then I'd get up and I'd walk out. I'd sit in church and ask God to forgive me for everything I'd done and to keep my faith up. Then I'd walk out of the church and I'd walk to the liquor store.

So I went to the Salvation Army and tried to learn more about spirituality. And I came back to Toronto and I got worse. There was no escape, there was no way out. So I drank, and when I drank, the feeling went away, but when I sobered up, it was there.

I was sitting in Allan Gardens one morning and this young lady was going from bench to bench and she had these pamphlets with scriptures from the Bible. She sat down and told me what she was like a year ago and what changed her life. I had a relationship with her and her husband for about three months. I used to go and meet with them and they would tell me different things about how they found spirituality. But I just couldn't grasp it. They tried hard, but I was getting worse. It was the conflict inside of me.

One day I was at the Friendship Centre and a guy I knew there said, "You want to come and help us? We need somebody to run the chain saw for us in Campbellville." We got down there, and they were holding one of these healing services for a certain person in Thunder Bay. They were having what they call a sweat lodge. They wanted me to cut the wood so they could heat up their rocks. They asked me if I wanted to participate. I said, "No, I never had anything to do with ... I don't know the first thing about it." "Well," they said, "you can stand around and listen anyway." The old medicine man said, "Just listen."

There was a little boy 8 years old there. They all went in to start the ceremony. He was sitting on a log and he kept watching me. Then he called me over. So I went over and sat with him and he said to me, "You don't understand what's going on in there, do you?" I said no. He said, "It's only a place – it's like a church, that's all it is. You go in there, you pray, you ask for forgiveness. But there's one thing," he said, "you have to remember to have faith and to believe." That struck me.

We sat there and talked about different things, and after everything was over we cleaned up, and he helped me. I went back two weeks later and I participated with them, and when I came out of that sweat lodge I was a totally different person.

I never learned much English. All I learned was the alphabet. I didn't learn how to spell or how to read. When I came out of that sweat lodge I came back to Toronto and I started picking up books and I started to read. I could understand what the writing was – I didn't have to look in the dictionary too much anymore. I could pick up the Bible and read it without having to close it with flusteration.

And I was able to see things more clearly. I didn't realize how negative I had been or how angry I had been in this world. I didn't realize how jealous I was. It was a tremendous turnaround.

I didn't know what to do with myself because I was so used to living a different sort of a life. I was used to living in the park and drinking with people and eating at the Brothers or at the Scott Mission or going to the Salvation Army for a bowl of soup. I had to turn the whole thing around and try to become a human being. I had to change my attitude, which was tremendously rotten.

I was riding on the subway one day and it was very crowded. I was getting off, and this woman got her handbag caught in my shoulder. When the door opened I went out and I was dragging this woman out with me because she was holding on to her purse. I undid the strap off my shoulder and stepped back on the train and held the doors so they wouldn't close – if I hadn't done that she would've had to wait for the next train.

She got on and I said, "I'm sorry." That's when I noticed my attitude was starting to change. I started saying more often, "Excuse me. I'm sorry." I learned to say thank you. There's some people would say thank you but they're sort of making fun of the word. To be able to say thank you and be sincere about it was something I had never done in my life.

I became a counsellor of alcoholics a year after I went to that sweat lodge. When I was counselling alcoholics, I tried to help people the best way I could. The clients weren't all alcoholics – some were inhalants, drug addicts. They would come to me and I would do my best to help them.

But I took sick after five or six years of it. I had several operations. For about two years I could hardly move around. And I wondered where I had lost my faith. I had no peace of mind. Two years ago I started the whole thing over again. I sat in my room for about a month and I thought about it and thought about it: "Where did I go wrong? Where did I go wrong?"

I had to let everything go. There are so many things I would like to have but I can't have them because they'll ruin my peace of mind. I don't like to go to the show because it's gonna ruin my peace of mind. I can't drink because it's gonna ruin my peace of mind. I can't have a relationship with a woman because it's gonna ruin my peace of mind. The only thing I can do is try to help other people, and that is the only way that my mind will sort of stabilize.

Those kids my wife had – there's two of them in Toronto and they come and see me every now and again. A year ago the second youngest girl called me. Said, "I'm in Toronto, where're you living? I'm coming down to see you." When I last saw her she had been only nine or ten years old. When she walked in the door she was a grown woman. She said, "I need – *I have to have* – an identity." I knew what was coming. I said, "Did your mother tell you?" She said, "Oh, she didn't say it in so many words, but I want to hear it from you."

I told her who her father was, and I told her what happened. Took me about an hour and a half to tell her. Now she's okay, she's got her identity, she feels much better. It had to be done. As soon as her brother heard about it, he was down here, and he went through the same thing. I still got three more to go.

My wife was here about three weeks ago. I went and met her at the hotel. We walked around Yonge Street for while, talked about different things. She wanted to know if I wanted to go back north. I said, "What's the use? I put you through enough. It wasn't you – it was me. I was never satisfied, I always needed that extra drink. That's probably the way it would be if I went back. You can come here and visit me any time you like. I can't go back fishing, or go out in the bush. It's the adjusting. The city of Toronto is my home now." It took me a long time – pretty near 50 years – to realize all the things I had done wrong. I'll never have enough time to make amends to the people I hurt. I can accept myself as I am today, and that took a long time, too. To be able to say, "Accept Lorne as Lorne is. Accept Lorne because he's an alcoholic. Accept Lorne because he's an Indian." These are the things that I could never accept. And today I can accept them.

I go to AA meetings and sometimes people come to me and they ask me different questions about different things. And I'll explain to them what it was like, what I went through. But I won't tell them what to do.

I was speaking one Saturday morning and there must have been 200 people there. I was sitting there trying to figure out what I would say. So I said a prayer before I went up there. They introduced me, I walked up there – it's a pulpit. I had no idea what I was gonna say.

But I said, "I am not gonna preach to you like they usually do up here." That sort of opened it up. I was watching everybody seated in front of me. When I mentioned the word God everybody sort of cringed, and I stopped and I said, "I see when I mention the word God a lot of you cringe. Do you really know what spirituality is? There's no lightning bolt gonna come down and hit you. It's only a relationship with God as you understand him. That's all it is. That's how simple it is. So there's no need to cringe."

AS I LISTEN _____

Lorne's story left me exhausted but full of hope. His life was so filled with ups and downs, victories and defeats, high hopes and utter despair. But it was an example of the incredible durability and resilience of human beings – how much they can go through and yet survive.

But Lorne did more than survive. He emerged as a wise man who learned much and was able to counsel others. People came to him for advice. He had resolved his tension between the culture in which he was raised and the culture he lived in. He also resolved the tension between his self-rejection and his longing for self-acceptance.

The road he followed to this resolution was a tortuous one. Lorne sank to the depths of despair time and again, and he couldn't find anything or anyone who responded to his cry for help. But he had a great genius for getting up and starting again, and for using broken material to build new structures. He emerges as a person of real dignity and nobility, one who could reflect with wisdom on the actions of others and himself.

AS I RESPOND

"I'm Not Good Enough - I Can't Make Babies"

Lorne has made me think about the concept of maleness and potency and creativity. In a way, I can identify with Lorne in his feeling of impotence when he finds that he can't make babies.

My wife and I had four children – she and I could make babies alright. But I realize now that there is more to potency than making babies. There is the whole concept of feeling that you are responsible for making things happen, and that if they don't happen, it's your fault. As a man I bought into the old stereotype that it was my responsibility to provide for my family. I assumed that when we got married my wife would quit her job (teaching music) and stay home, look after the house and the children and be a partner to me in my work. She would use her special abilities only as a hobby. I don't remember saying all this, or even thinking it; I guess I just assumed it.

Unfortunately, my wife accepted the stereotype, too. When I was doing post-graduate studies in New York City, my wife studied the pipe organ. (She was an accomplished pianist before we were married.) I remember her teacher, an outstanding New York organist, saying to me with a smile, but with a depth of meaning that escaped me at the time: "I don't know whether I can forgive you for robbing the world of an outstanding organist."

Years later, when the children were grown and more or less independent, she did break out on her own and create music, art and poetry of a most imaginative kind. It was very late in her life (she died of cancer at age 59) before I began to see what she could conceive.

At first I was somewhat jealous of these "conceptions" of hers. They didn't come from me. They were from other people, poets, artists, musicians. I resented them. I resented the time she spent with them and did not spend with me. Only gradually did I acknowledge her work as valuable. Only slowly did I see it as a part of our partnership. These works of hers, conceived by her partnership with others, were works I could not have inspired in her. Jealous, bewildered and feeling inferior, I left her to them, and continued to immerse myself in my work. It was a kind of escape, somewhat like Lorne's alcoholism – but perhaps worse, because I called it dedication to God's work.

Lorne's humility, his realization that he could learn to rejoice in the children his wife bore by another man and take responsibility for them, even give them an identity and find enjoyment in them, opens up a wider, deeper concept of what it means for a husband and wife to "have children." Any meaningful partnership should produce something more than concrete, visible progeny. It should be, and can be, very creative and productive, provided the partners aren't hung up on a particular role they must play or a particular product they must conceive.

As I think back, some of the most creative times my wife and I had together were when we played and sang together late into the night. Many years later, after her death, one of our sons sat down with me and a liturgical dancer to pore over the story of Ezekiel and the valley of dry bones. Together we created a worship service around that biblical passage. I think my son and I were aware that we were engaged in the kind of creativity my wife had pioneered. It allowed people to create what they could – the dancer, the musician and the preacher – and to see the outcome not only as something greater than any one of us could have *done* by ourselves but as something greater than any one of us could have *conceived* by ourselves.

Creativity is thwarted when any one person feels he or she has to take full responsibility for the outcome. That is what Lorne at first failed to see. He thought that if he and his wife had no babies, it was his fault. That made him feel inferior. He could not bear that kind of feeling indefinitely. Nobody can. So he turned to alcohol. If he had seen it as *their* problem, he and his wife might have talked about it together and arranged to adopt children. But as it was, there was no alternative for him but to leave in shame and anger.

Other people feel that a certain preconceived product must emerge. That is where I fell down. I enjoyed hearing my wife play the piano and organ. I enjoyed our playing and singing together. But the kinds of creations she was making with other people were strange to me. I found avant garde music, art and poetry, foreign, even objectionable. I was not open to learning about new and different forms of artistic expression, especially when "fathered" by others.

Such prejudices stifle creativity. The prophet Ezekiel found closed minds in his people. They were living in captivity in Babylon, far from their beloved homeland. All they could think of was the day God would overthrow their captors and lead them back to Jerusalem and its beautiful temple. Ezekiel warned them against this kind of hope. When the news came that Jerusalem and the temple had been destroyed they sank into despair. Ezekiel compares them to a valley of dry bones and believes that God is challenging them with the question, "Can these bones live again?" Can we dare to hope for a new kind of creation out of the death of an old dream?

The people in their captivity had stopped singing. They said, "How can we sing the Lord's song in a strange land?" But in a sense that is what we are all called to do.

Now I am remarried, and I am trying to continue learning. The old male stereotype is gradually changing, as is the female stereotype. My wife keeps her own name. She has her own job. She has her own talents, quite different from Pat's. It is too late for us to have children, but we are finding ways to create things together.

"I Decided to Make an Amend"

Lorne helps me to understand more deeply the meaning of forgiveness and reconciliation. When he decides to buy a house for his wife and children and set up an education fund, he doesn't say, "I decided to forgive my wife." He says instead, "I decided to make an amend."

Lorne reminds me of Cain in some ways. Cain was jealous because God had accepted his brother Abel's sacrifice, but not his. It was patently unjust, unfair. Cain was angry. God warned him to be careful of his anger – it could have devastating consequences if it got out of control. But Cain wouldn't listen. He decided to repay injustice with violence. He murdered his brother. As a result, he became a wanderer on the earth.

Lorne felt unjustly dealt with. Somebody else fathered his wife's children. Someone took advantage of his impotence. He was penalized for something he couldn't help. He reacted with fury. He left his wife and drowned himself in alcohol. Like Cain, he became a wanderer, going from place to place, from job to job.

But as he reflected, Lorne saw that it was reconciliation, not the establishment of blame, that was needed.

Lorne's decision to make an amend didn't repair everything. Reconciliation does not mean that everything that has happened can be fixed. Lorne reminds me of God's treatment of the human race after it had violated its covenant with God. God regretted making humans and destroyed them and the earth with a flood. But then God repented, and formed a new covenant with Noah and his wife and their descendants. God recognized that human beings with the power of free will inevitably abuse it.

God would have to get along with imperfection. God formed a new covenant with imperfect people and set a rainbow in the sky to remind *God* – not them – that whatever happened, destruction of the guilty is never a solution to a breach of trust. Nor is mere forgiveness sufficient in itself.

When a marriage breaks and ends in divorce, often there is a lot of guilt and remorse on both sides. The divorce proceedings often aggravate hard feelings and create a desire for revenge. Few people feel good about leaving the situation that way. But someone has to take the initiative and try to salvage something from the wreckage. It is not enough to say, Oh, I forgive the other person, but there is nothing that can be done about it. Usually there is something that can be done, and forgiveness is the source of creative action.

There is a sense, too, in which we can forgive circumstances, or fate, or God, for bad things that happen to us – things like illness or the death of a loved one or the loss of a job, things that are unjust, and to which we react with anger and bitterness. We must learn to forgive fate.

Getting to know people with AIDS has provided many examples for me of people making amends in the way Lorne did. Some understandably lash out at the tragic injustice of life. But a significant number get beyond that. Many insist that they are not people with AIDS but people *living* with AIDS. One, a social worker, counsels other people with AIDS and speaks in schools and at public gatherings, educating people about the disease. Some go out of their way to be reconciled to their parents, who rejected them because they are gay. Some bear their suffering and their fate with such good humor and quiet faith that they are an inspiration to all who know them. It is as though the worst fate can do to them has brought out the best in them.

All this gives me a new understanding of God and God's kingdom. Perhaps the kingdom of God is not a new Eden, where everything is perfect, but an amazing collage produced by God with scarred individuals and flawed societies and leftover remnants. Perhaps hell will be the place where only the perfect can go, while heaven will be reserved for the halt, the poor, the broken and the sinners. One more blessed heresy occurs to me: What if even God is not perfect? Has perfection been overrated?

"It Was a Tremendous Turnaround"

All my life I have had to struggle with the statement, "You can't change human nature." Yet that is exactly what religion is supposed to do. I have always been an idealist – probably often a rather naive idealist. I have believed and preached that society can be changed and that people can be changed by the power and grace of God. But I have to ask: "Has it happened to me?"

My own conversion came when I was a young teenager. I hadn't had any of the traumatic experiences Lorne had. I never reached the point of utter desperation. But I was closest to God when I was faced with something too big for me or with a burden too difficult to bear. In those moments, I was amazed at how utter need preceded a sense of the real presence of God. I was also amazed at how the burning agony of that need was like a purifying fire that purged my faith of all its alloys and left the shining ore of simple truth.

After Lorne has tried this and tried that, a little boy persuades him to go into the sweat lodge and not to be afraid. Why? Because it's simple and basic. As the boy put it, "You go in there, you pray, you ask forgiveness. But there's one thing, you have to remember to have faith and to believe."

I remember standing by the open grave of my wife and wondering, "Is there life after death? Will we still be married? What kind of relationship will it be?" I stood by the grave of our retarded daughter and asked, "Will she be normal over there? What would be 'normal' for her?" Then a voice within me asks, "Why not leave all that to God?"

What intrigues me about Lorne's conversion is that it is a mixture of intellectual and emotional change. He can now read and think clearly. But he can also read himself and his attitudes clearly – and do something about them. In recent years we have heard a lot about holistic medicine and religion. Lorne demonstrates clearly what that is. His conversion takes place in the fires of a sweat lodge. And the result? He is able to say, for the first time, "Thank you" and "I'm sorry" and be sincere about it. "Thank you" and "I'm sorry" are outward-looking, not inward-looking words.

My own experience of being born again was motivated, even at the age of 14, by a desire to be saved. But I found that one's individual salvation is not enough. In fact, I realized that to be saved could be the opposite of salvation: it could be a religious form of self-preservation. It could also be the religious version of the secular desire to look after oneself regardless of what was happening to others. Like Lorne, I learned how fulfilling it is to help someone else.

Lorne helps me to reflect on my own pilgrimage or spiritual journey. I used to think that conversion was a once-in-a-lifetime, mountaintop experience that changed everything. I know now that the spiritual journey leads us over a varied terrain. There are mountaintops, where there is a sudden view that is tremendously exciting and where we make decisions about the next leg of our journey. But there are also dusty plains and dark valleys. All add to the religious experience. The valleys might be where the visions of the mountaintop are translated into specific actions and attitudes.

Another thing I realized as I listen to Lorne is that salvation is both an intensely personal and an intensely social act. When he went into the sweat lodge, Lorne was preoccupied with his own overwhelming need. But after he emerged he began to help other alcoholics.

I thought my decision had been a very personal one, but it, too, was participatory. It was stimulated by participating in acts of study and worship with others. The great theologian Reinhold Niebuhr said, "It may be that if we cannot all be saved, we cannot be saved at all." I think Lorne would agree.

The feeling that comes with age and experience is that it is not so easy to change people or the world, let alone myself. So I stand, as it were, outside the sweat lodge, asking questions, considering the odds, while others go in and sweat out their answers. Perhaps I need, like Lorne, to talk with an 8-year-old and let him remind me that the ingredients of change remain simple, though not easy. It's not so much a matter of reason or wisdom, but of willingness to risk and change.

In retrospect, I realize that I have indeed made some changes in my life. When our fourth child was born, she had Down's syndrome. It was a shock to my wife and me. In those days, 30 years ago, there was much less knowledge about handicapped children, and very little public acceptance and provision for them.

As well, my wife had only recently recovered from a long and deep bout of depression. The doctor who delivered the child was afraid of the effect her retardation might have on my wife. He felt that we should place the child in a home for the sake of my wife's health. When my wife was told about the child's handicaps, she went numb and was incapable of making a decision. I had to make it.

Very reluctantly I followed the doctor's advice and took our new baby to a special home some distance away. But I could not rest with the decision. Was I abandoning our child? How was my action expressing my love? Nobody I talked to seemed able to help. I found that my well-intentioned friends seemed to be living in a different world. The pressure built until one day, alone in the vestry of my church, I threw myself on the floor and wept and cried to God. The answer that came was quite simple: "What did you name your child?" We had named her Grace after my sister and my wife's sister. That was before we had known of her handicap. Now the question seemed to be, "What does grace mean?" It means, of course, God's unconditional and unmerited love for us. Why, then, could I not offer grace to Grace? In that moment, I saw Grace as I should have seen her from the beginning, as our child, as one of our family. To make a long story short, we brought Grace home, her mother responded with amazing health and strength, the family was strengthened – and I was "converted."

Some day I hope to be permitted to participate in a native sweat lodge. Before I met Lorne and heard his story I would have been very apprehensive, feeling that I had no common ground on which to approach such a ceremony. But talking to Lorne helped me to see a similarity. Lorne received grace to accept himself in spite of what he regarded as handicaps: his native origins, his alcoholism, his misdeeds. I received grace to accept one of my own, whom I had held at arm's length, and in so doing experienced a deeper and more complete understanding of God and of God's love for us all. Like Lorne, I had experienced a complete turnaround.

5

JENNIFER
The Struggle with Suffering

Jennifer is a young woman of 27 years of age. She is of slight build and dresses with taste and a certain meticulousness. She is very fair, and her face is rather pale from her years of suffering. When I talked with her she had been depressed for three years. Her depression has not lifted since. She has had the very best medical attention, but to no avail. In spite of her incredible anguish she managed, with determination and great effort, to complete her bachelor's degree from the University of Toronto with high distinction. When I got to know Jennifer I realized that she needed someone who would be her friend – someone who would see her regularly and be able to listen with sensitivity and understanding. Fortunately, I was able to find such a person, Josephine. Jennifer pays high tribute to Josephine in her story, and I have included some of Josephine's reflections. I did not ask Jennifer to tell me the story of her life from the beginning; instead I asked her to tell me what it was like to be so depressed, and how she had coped. She began by telling about a rare period of four days when the depression had inexplicably lifted.

Tell me what it was like when you had those four days of liberation.

It's a hard feeling to put into words. I simply woke up and felt an incredible sense of inner peace. The anxiety that I had experienced just vanished, and I felt as though I was going to live again as a normal person, not having to force myself to do things, trying to function in spite of feeling totally overwhelmed by the world, feeling so anxious that I would be totally debilitated. I felt as though that black curtain had been drawn away. I saw the world completely differently.

Along with that is an incredible sense of urgency – to do something. I think it comes from the fact that these periods when it's lifted have never been sustained. And so there is this incredible sense of urgency to do something you've wanted to do for years and never been able to do. It's somewhat overwhelming, because you don't know where to start. I almost have to shake myself and say, "Is this really true or am I just dreaming?" And you think, "So I made it.

I managed to sustain myself to the end. I survived." And that sense of urgency: "I have to live now because I have the gift of life and I can't waste a minute of it because it's so precious and I fought so hard for it, struggled so hard for it."

Is there a fear that it's going to go away any minute?

I think it's there unconsciously. Consciously, you're still caught up in the incredible sense of feeling better. When I'm depressed I have a distorted idea that I'm not very attractive. But I would look in the mirror and I would see someone totally different – I mean, it's the same person but a transformation had taken place. I would look at myself and I would say: "I like that. That's me. That's okay." There's a sense of self-acceptance, whereas when I'm sick there's a struggle to accept the illness and to somehow integrate it into myself. But when I feel better there is somehow a gentler kind of acceptance, of peace.

Somehow I'm able to see myself in a much broader context than when I'm sick. When I'm sick it's very much an hour-to-hour or a day-to-day struggle. I can't see the broader picture. But those four days were a gift. They were also an affirmation that I can feel better. Because I think there is always part of me that keeps saying: "Will I know what it feels like to be better? Is that ever going to happen? Or have I simply learned to be sick?" There is a theory of depression that speaks of the "learned helplessness" model. I've always thought that was ridiculous in my case, but I guess there's a part of me that wonders, Have I learned to be depressed, and is that something I have to unlearn? Those four days show me that it isn't learned helplessness, that I am able to feel well. But it's not something I can control or dictate.

When I'm ill I can't see anything else – I can't see any of the accomplishments I have had in my life. All I see and feel is a sense of failure, inadequacy. I think for a lot of people who suffer from chronic depression there is no hope. They don't have anything to cling to. But I have been blessed with a hope, a faith, a sustaining vision, that my depression will end in time. I don't know how long it will take, I don't know what will be the circumstances that will make it go away. But it will happen. My task is to survive, to fight on, to recognize those times when there is no point in fighting, when I must accept that it's really bad and try to pull myself together. And then when it lightens somewhat, to recommence the journey, to live with as much dignity as possible.

And to lead as normal a life as possible. That's very hard to do. At times it's impossible. You can't go on as though everything's all right. I've never been able to do that. So I try to find people like Josephine who can give me their time and their love. Because I think those are healing powers, just as much as medication is, in my case. It's that human touch that makes the journey bearable. She touched my life in a very special way. She was there for me. Helped me to accept myself, to accept the pain, because there's a great temptation to try to deny it, to look away from it and say, "This really isn't happening."

For years, during my earlier depressions, I went to bed and looked at the wall for months on end. If someone asked me if I was sick, I denied it. I couldn't accept it. When my father attempted to get me some kind of psychiatric help I insisted that he was the one with the problem. It was only in my later depressions that I knew I needed some kind of help.

Josephine really helped. She came every week, and that commitment was like saying to me: "You're an important person. You matter. And it matters to me whether you get through this." She had such a gentle manner. She would be there with me, quietly, even if I wasn't able to carry on much of a conversation. She was sensitive to my need for her presence, even if I wasn't able to interact with her. Sometimes I'd retreat into a kind of shell. I'd need the support, but it's hard to interact with someone. I'm forever grateful that you found her for me. You couldn't have chosen a better person.

We are fortunate that it turned out so well. You meant a tremendous amount to her, too. I'm convinced that this decision she's made, to leave her job and work with mentally handicapped adults, is partly due to you. I hope you can take some comfort and affirmation from that. But tell me what it's like when you're in the depths. What are you feeling then?

An incredible sense of loneliness. I feel so alone, as though the whole world has abandoned me. The only thing that sustains me is that I feel closer to God then than I do at any other time. Somehow he is with me there, in my pain, when no one can really be there with me. I feel as though my whole life is shipwrecked, it's totally shattered and fallen apart. I sob almost uncontrollably. Often I just lie on the floor, because you can't fall off the floor. I feel there's no point in going on. No point in continuing. There's nothing good about me, there's nothing worthwhile or meaningful in my life. I have totally irrational thoughts. I know these are distorted thoughts, I know they are sick thoughts, but they are still there, and no amount of trying to talk myself out of it is going to change it. I lose all sense of perspective. All I can see is that moment. Being deprived of any perspective is an incredible handicap.

I feel abandoned – again it's an irrational thought. I often feel as though it would be better for my family if I just wasn't here any more, because I seem to cause them increasingly more pain. The only thing I can hold on to, something I can clutch, is my faith. It's there inside me. It cannot be destroyed by the negativeness of the experience. It's very real to me, very powerful, and very sustaining. I find music quieting. It accompanies me through those really hard times.

Is there any particular kind of music that helps?

Choral music. St. John Passion. St. Matthew Passion. Bach's Mass in B Minor. It's as though, in some of those pieces, the pain I experience is translated. I can't translate it into words but I can hear a piece of music and say, "That expresses what I'm feeling." That's very reassuring. There's a great need to know that pain can be translated into something comprehensible. You've seen me in some of my worst states.

You also have a feeling at times of tremendous anger and rebellion. At the same time as you have faith in God, you can be angry.

Yes. I ask, "Why is this happening? Why does it go on without any help? The doctors don't seem to be able to do a whole lot. All they can give me is symptomatic treatment. If I sob uncontrollably they can give me something to calm me down. If I'm totally debilitated by the anxiety they can give me something to quiet it, but they can't get at the root. They can't eradicate the feeling.

There's a sense of frustration. Why can't people do something? Primarily, why can't *I* do something? Because I continually blame myself. What is it that I do wrong? I don't believe I'm an inherently bad person. I can't make it go away. All I can try to do is accept the feelings and try to carry on, but I can't understand why. I don't think there is a reason. I don't think God wants this thing any more than I want it – it's part of my existence.

I feel a tremendous sense of powerlessness because I can't change it, and I see how destructive it is. I think, Why should this shatter my life? There's so much I could offer the world. So many positive things I could contribute. Why is that being mortgaged? But your words about Josephine make me feel that it hasn't all been loss – that even in my moments of despair and pain I have been able to enrich someone else's life.

Faith is the only thing that sustains me. Nothing else. The medication helps a little bit – it has prevented me from ending my own life and for that I'm grateful, but it doesn't reach me. All it does is deaden my feelings. The pain, the cutting – it's just like a knife that goes through my whole body. No medication can dull that.

I see my life as a journey. One of the things this illness has taught me is how precious life is and how precious time is. I think we take time for granted. We don't really pay attention to the passing of time. But during my illness there are periods when I realize how precious time is, because life has in some ways been taken away from me. I exist physically, but there is no quality to my life. In those four days when I felt better, there was a sense of urgency to go out into the world and to give and to truly live with purpose and meaning, because there has been such a long period in my life when I haven't been able to really live.

Eventually I want to be able to integrate these periods of pain and to recognize the change that will have taken place in me. I used to always want to be my old self again. My father would sometimes say, "You know, the day will come, dear, when you'll be your old self again." That isn't really true – I will never be my old self again. What I have experienced and what I have survived will alter my personhood for ever. You are never the same again. So I see life as a journey.

It's a journey because it's a series of unending changes. There are people who don't like change, who fear it because change is inherently stressful. But for me there's also a sense of curiosity. I wonder how the future will unfold and what role my experiences will play in that future.

There is a desire to try to stuff all this pain in some corner of my being and lock it up. But at a deeper level I realize I will never be able to do that. What I have experienced will affect who I am and what I do for the rest of my life. I think you have to have tasted pain and disappointment, failure, too, to be able to reach out to other people. People have reached out to me in my periods of tribulation.

I have a dream. I don't know how realistic it is, but I would very much like to establish some kind of support system for people in the community who suffer from mental illness. I have demonstrated that it is possible to exist outside of an institution in spite of an overwhelming handicap. But there is no support in the community. I've often thought, if only I had somewhere to go, maybe just to sleep overnight – somewhere where there would be people that cared, people that could look after my physical needs. Because quite often I'm not well enough to cook, so I don't eat. I can't get off the floor. I can't decide whether I should open a can of beans or have a tuna-fish salad. I've often wished there was some place I could go to have a cup of coffee and just be surrounded by people. I live by myself, and that's very hard when you're depressed, to be by yourself.

I would like to try to develop a house or a place where people could come, where there would be qualified counsellors. There are people who, when I have been suicidal, would say, "You can't really feel this way. This is ridiculous." They deny the way I feel. I need a place where there would be people who understand my kind of disability. I don't belong locked up in a mental hospital. I would die spiritually and emotionally. I've been in a mental hospital and it was more traumatic than the illness.

I think people can survive in a sheltered situation. I can work but it's very difficult for me to work in a normal job. Some days I might work two hours here and two hours somewhere else. Some days I might not be able to work at all. Other days I will be able to work more. I don't fit into a certain mold. That doesn't mean that I'm permanently unemployable.

I spent seven years fighting with the university. They refused to accept my psychiatric disability. I would petition to have courses done on an independent study basis because I was unable to attend lectures on a regular basis. It's only in the past five years that university buildings have been made accessible to people with physical disabilities. Maybe in another 10 or 15 years people with psychiatric disabilities will also be encouraged and be able to pursue studies.

Maybe I should become a lawyer, an advocate for social justice. I feel very strongly that the mental health system has to change. The state's not going to be able to afford to keep all those people in institutions. The community is going to have to shoulder some of that responsibility. I'm not advocating that we open the doors of mental hospitals and let everybody walk around the streets, but I feel that some people are in there who wouldn't have to be there if there were ways of finding support for them.

If you were to meet a person who is going through what you've gone through, and are still going through, what would you say to them?

I would say that I can share their pain, that I can understand some of that pain, but I can't make it go away for them. I can be present with them and I can give them my love and I can share my faith.

How would you do that?

Perhaps by sharing with them those times when my faith was all that sustained me. I have found strength and courage and hope at times when I felt there was no hope. I found strength to manage from one day to the next. The fact that I'm able to sit here today is a testimony to that. But it wasn't something I was able to do all by myself.

You said that you used to think you'd like to be your old self, but that's neither possible nor desirable. What's different about the self you now have?

I think I have a more realistic view of who I am as a person, what my limitations are. I think I also have a much stronger sense of the value of human life, because that life is a gift of God, and it's nearly been taken away from me on many occasions.

I sense also that my life has more purpose and more direction than it had because I've been forced to look at life straight on. It's been a painful experience, looking at it straight on. I had previously glanced at it and kept right on walking by. I think I'm a more compassionate person. I think I have more patience with myself and people around me.

You've been three years in depression and aren't out of it yet. When you look to the future, do you look with hope or with dread?

I hate to look at it with dread – I might just as well dig my own grave right now. I look to it with hope because I feel I have come to accept that there is never going to be a cure for my illness. I hope it will be controlled, that with medication the depressions will be lessened in severity and shortened in duration.

Part of me wants to live. I don't know how to explain it, but even in those times when I have really been on the brink of utter desolation and despair, there is part of me that holds on to life with a tenacity that at times surprises me. That's something that I don't think will ever be destroyed, and as long as I have that and as long as I have my faith, there is hope. There is something to live for. I believe that God will provide ways and means to help me through these times, just as he's given me you and Josephine. If I am willing to let go of my life enough to let him take over – I don't know how he is going to provide. It may not be in ways that I would like. But he will provide.

Yes, there is dread and there is apprehension. That apprehension will always be there, as will the scars of these three years, but I will also be able to say that I made it through, and I'll be able to take some credit. I have accomplished something. It wasn't exactly what I wanted – by now I should have been well along to a Ph.D., which is what I wanted to do. But maybe, if I look at my whole life, that isn't as important as it seemed at the time. Maybe there were other accomplishments and other challenges that were more important.

I look to the future with apprehension but also with a sense that I will make it. I don't know how, but I will. I've made it this far.

Response To Jennifer By Her Friend, Josephine

Josephine is a person I asked to be a friend to Jennifer. She is about 10 or 15 years older than Jennifer and she was working in a responsible administrative position. She proved to be an ideal person for Jennifer. She visited with her faithfully every week. She's a good listener, and a person who could identify exceptionally well with Jennifer, partly because she has had some experience with depression herself.

After two years of befriending Jennifer, Josephine decided to leave her job to go to work with mentally handicapped adults.

I asked her to describe her relationship with Jennifer.

Two years ago you asked me to give Jennifer a call and it was a very easy thing to do. I phoned her and we went out for coffee. I just listened to her talk about her days or her weeks.

At the beginning I wanted to interject. There were certain emotions going on inside me she would bring up, not particularly pleasant emotions, and I would have to bite my tongue sometimes. But as time went on it got easier, and I realized there was so much pain there. I also began to notice that as you listen and if you really concentrate on a person's pain, you begin to feel something moving inside you, too, that feels good. I was reading Jean Vanier at the time, about dealing with people and their suffering, and perhaps that was in the back of my mind.

I began to feel that it was almost a holy experience at times, just to be there. You don't say anything, but you're helping with their pain in some ways. It doesn't get you down – I would go away feeling good about it. Feeling something inside my chest was opening up. So when she would say to me, "Oh, thank you so much," I would say, "But Jennifer, you don't know what you're doing for me." I can't explain it. I tried to explain it to her. I know it's a bit unusual.

She was careful not to impose or to demand too much. She'd talk about her day and what was bothering her, the anguish, the anxiety. She talked a lot about her medication, her visits to the doctors. She went to so many doctors in her pain – her teeth, her bones, her feet. She talked about the psychiatrist, the various drugs and what they were doing to her body. About her friends – and that was sad, because as time went on they moved on to other things. Her family, her relationship with her sister, mother, father. At the end of each session I felt – well, I was able to make a difference to her. Being with her in her suffering, I, too, am growing. We talked about what it means to be a reject in this society, for whatever reason. I think we all feel that we are rejects at one time or another. Or we feel that we're weak or vulnerable, or somehow an outsider.

Society has put so many demands on a person like Jennifer. She's supposed to measure up in this way and that way and have a job and a good career and be married and have this, have that. Even if she succeeds quite well, given her handicap, she's never going to be happy because the demands will always be there.

I think being with Jennifer influenced my decision to change jobs. I thought about why Jennifer is like she is. Why is there suffering? Why is there pain? And I have no answer. It's very upsetting. It's part of the human condition. And what's the point of it all? Her suffering is just mind-boggling.

Jennifer made me more sensitive. I think just being with her made me realize that you do feel the presence of God when you are sharing someone's suffering. That's part of what Jean Vanier is saying: that if you are with those who are marginal people in society, those who have handicaps, you will in some way find the mystery of Jesus there.

AS I LISTEN

Jennifer's story was powerful because it dramatized some of the ultimate questions of life. It raised profound questions of faith. How can there be a God of love and compassion who allows such pain? What can I possibly have done to deserve this? Where can I possibly find resources to face something that is destroying me daily and for which there seems to be no hope of cure or even relief?

It was humbling to sit in the presence of someone who was asking these questions out of their own excruciating pain. But, as Josephine said, there was something mysteriously inspiring about it, too. It is because we are in the presence of the ultimate.

Jennifer was aware of this. There was something almost saintly about her as she tried to transform her pain into something transcendent and holy. I was left feeling in one sense helpless, but in another sense privileged to share, even in a small way, her journey.

AS I RESPOND

"An Incredible Sense of Inner Peace"

It is heartbreaking to think of how much Jennifer wrings out of four days of peace during three long years of depression. It is hard to imagine a person daring to hope and plan again after years of despair and hopelessness. It is heartbreaking because it seems so cruel that she should have to be plunged again into darkness after such a tiny glimpse of light.

And yet I realize that for Jennifer the four days of peace are not a mere respite from the harsh reality of her ongoing depression. Those four days *are* reality – the ultimate reality, in which the reality of her depression is put into perspective and is seen as *not* ultimate. She sees herself as she really is – not as someone defeated by circumstances but as one who has survived and who has a purpose to fulfil. She sees herself not as an ugly, unlovely person but as someone she can accept and love. She sees her condition not as something she has brought on herself and for which she should feel constantly guilty, not as something characteristic of her, but as a mystery that, while it cannot be explained and may never go away, is something that she can learn to live with. It may even, in some strange way, deepen her understanding of herself, of others, and of life itself.

I am moved by the depth and power of Jennifer's insights, gleaned from a moment of release in a history of bondage. But as I think about it, there is a sense in which I live by the strength of such moments, too. The moments may not be as brief nor as infrequent, and the strength I gain from them might not be as concentrated and distilled as it is for Jennifer. For the most part, I receive sufficient affirmation from others and from the work I do to be able to accept myself and my lot in life. But as a minister in the church I have always dealt with intangibles. There are times when it is hard to see any concrete results from the efforts of 40 years. Recently I visited some tiny communities in northern Saskatchewan where I had served as a young student minister. Of the eight places where I had conducted services, only one building remained where regular worship was held. The rest had disappeared completely or were in various stages of decay. It made me wonder. Was what I did in those years of no account? I remembered the verse from the Psalms: "The wind passeth over it and it is gone, and the place thereof shall know it no more." Experiences like that make me ask, Has my whole life been built on an illusion? What if there is no God? It is not hard to look at the world and wonder whether it is any different from what it was centuries ago. Are we all, perhaps, as the psalmist said, just like the grass of the field, which springs up today and tomorrow is gone? Are all my hopes and the hopes I have preached just so much positive thinking? Mere studied optimism? A form of whistling in the dark to keep up my courage and the courage of others?

These moods are not frequent and do not last long, but they help me to understand something of how Jennifer feels in her depression. I realize my faith is dependent on moments of rare clarity, when I see truth. Some of the brightest moments happen when I meet someone like Jennifer. Here she is, a talented young woman of 27, cursed with the blight of an almost unceasing depression. But in a brief respite she manages to catch an entirely different view of herself, her purpose in life, and of the world itself.

Jennifer helps me to bet on her faith. And if I'm wrong, I'd sooner be in her company than with those who were right.

"An Incredible Sense of Loneliness"

Talking with Jennifer was always a very painful, exhausting experience. I felt that I was out of my depth. I felt she had a desperate need for hope, and yet I was afraid to offer anything that might seem like a glib or cheap hope. What prospect was there that she would be cured of her depression? And without a cure, could I afford to speak of hope? The other thing she needed was understanding. How could I, who had never been depressed in the way Jennifer is, pretend to understand what she is suffering?

I recalled the depression of my wife, Pat. It came and went for most of our married life. Pat's depression crippled her. For long periods of time, she was unable to do what she was so superbly equipped to do. For more than a year she was unable to be a mother to our two children. I was a single parent for a while. Pat had to be hospitalized, and while she was away the children would wake up in the night and call out for her. They were too young to understand where their mother was. It gave me a small taste of what it must be like for a single parent to try to explain to young children what has happened to the marriage, why the other parent is not there.

There is a loneliness that depression brings. It brings it both to the depressed and to those who live with them. I can understand, somewhat, how Jennifer feels – to be depressed is to be marginalized. When you are depressed you can't really think of anything but yourself and your agony. That cuts you off from others. Pat said to me one day when I was visiting her at the hospital: "You might as well forget about me. Just look after yourself and the children." I was appalled. But talking with Jennifer gave me a better understanding as to why Pat might have said that. She felt so cut off from reality – so alienated from the world and her husband and children – that it made sense to retreat into her own lonely world. Depression affects loved ones as it affects the depressed. It cuts you off from the normal conversation, sharing and demonstration of affection that is so vital to a relationship.

Pat was a superb musician. The sound of music was the characteristic sound of our home. But at times Pat felt incapable of using her talents. The piano fell silent. She could not even bear to hear music. A pall fell over our house. Shock treatments brought her no relief, and she cried uncontrollably every time I visited her in the hospital.

Depression reaches out its tentacles and threatens to strangle all who love the depressed. I could see why Jennifer's friends – and even some members of her own family – had withdrawn. People have to retreat in order to survive. They can't go on indefinitely with such a feeling of helplessness.

I did find ways of helping Pat, at least to some degree. In the first place, I knew it was important to be with her, especially because she had "released" me from what she felt was a burden. I felt it was important for me to keep saying to my wife, "I love you. I think you are beautiful. The children are waiting for you to come home from the hospital. They need you. They miss you. They love you, too. Home is just not home without you." Pat found that hard to believe in her depression, but I think she wanted to hear it anyway. It seemed such an obvious fact to me that I am afraid I did not say it as often as I should have. But I remember that saying it, knowing it was true, helped me, too.

Such things provide some kind of perspective for depressed persons. They think they are worthless, and that, since no cure is in sight, they might as well be dead. Jennifer's few days of remission restored her perspective. She could look in the mirror and see that she really was a beautiful human being, and she could feel that life could be very worthwhile.

When Jennifer called me on the phone, as she did when she got really depressed, I learned that it was important, first of all, to listen to her pain. She needed to tell someone how terrible the pain was. How helpless she felt. How lonely she was. And to cry out against God for letting the pain go on and on. It was important to take these cries seriously.

Jennifer sometimes asked me if my wife had such feelings about herself. I assured her that she did. And did my wife ever recover from such feelings? Yes, I replied, she did, although she had to struggle with her depression for most of her life.

I would also talk about the fact that Jennifer was one of a great number of people throughout history who have had to struggle with suffering. It is the subject of the whole Book of Job in the Old Testament. Job asks many of the questions Jennifer asks. Musicians, writers and artists who speak out of their pain find a form of release and make a great contribution to suffering humanity. Sometimes Jennifer could say that through her suffering she had become a better person, a more sensitive and understanding person, a more real person. I told Jennifer I thought her suffering was unjust, and that I believed God thought it was unjust, too. Why God did not relieve it is one of the great mysteries of life. But I said I believed God was suffering with her, and was just as anxious as she was that she be healed.

We talked about the difference between being "healed" and being "cured." Healing is the grace and strength we are given so that we can live with our suffering. Being cured means having the pain removed. I was not trying to avoid the tragedy of her suffering, but to open the possibility of her being able to use it creatively. Although God did not seem to be responding to her, God was nevertheless with her, day and night. I believe we are all created by God, in the image of God, and that God does not create ugly, worthless human beings.

Jennifer seemed open to hearing such things, and it was helpful for me to say them. I believe these things to be true, and saying them to someone who so desperately needed to know she was loved, that there was something to live for, helped me to believe them all the more deeply. I would tell Jennifer I was praying for her, and I asked her to pray for me. She assured me that she was praying for me and my family. I found that very moving. It was a sign of spiritual health, even in the depths of her illness.

I thought again about Job. In his failure to find any reason or sense in the awful suffering he was enduring, all Job asked for was some voice in the darkness that would tell him his suffering was observed – that there was someone out there. "If only I knew how to find God," he cries. "Then I should learn what answer God would give, and find out what God had to say." But there is no answer.

I had never thought of Job's suffering in terms of loneliness. But listening to Jennifer, I realized that the essence of Job's suffering was the utter loneliness of it. His closest friends mouthed well-intentioned platitudes that trivialized his pain. His wife said, "Curse God and die." Job was left with the feeling that no one – not even God – knows or cares about what we are going through. We are made for each other. We are made for God. When we have no others and no God, life becomes unbearable.

Job is grateful when God finally speaks to him. God gives no explanation for Job's suffering. God speaks to Job in tones that make Job feel understood and not alone. God has given Jennifer no answers. But as she kneels on the floor of her apartment and listens to music, the music of suffering, the St. John Passion and the St. Matthew Passion, she feels as though her pain is translated into something comprehensible.

When God has spoken out of the whirlwind, Job says, "I have spoken of great things which I have not understood, things too wonderful for me to know. I knew of thee then only by report, but now I see thee with my own eyes."

Do any of us experience the reality of the presence of God unless we go through something like Jennifer's loneliness? Such suffering backs our souls right up against the wall. We feel there has to be a God or we will die. And somehow we don't die, because God is there. Perhaps that's what Josephine sensed when she listened to Jennifer. She began to feel it was almost a holy experience at times, just to be there.

6

NORA
The Struggle with Death

Nora is a very attractive woman in her late thirties. She has an intelligent face and a lithe figure and an animated way of speaking. I visited her in the living room of her comfortable home in Vancouver a month after her 19-year-old son had been drowned in a freak accident. He was her only child, and she was still in a state of shock. But the event had also seemed to give her an unusually clear perspective.

I was born in Regina, Saskatchewan, to a very strict Catholic family. My father was an alcoholic. My brother and I have been left with a lot of problems stemming from that shaky foundation.

As a child I believed quite naturally and simply in God, not that I thought a great deal about it. We always had the catechism at school, and the nuns and the priests and the Mass every Sunday. I was particularly moved by the majesty of the Mass, and the transcendental atmosphere. My spirit felt touched by the pageantry. But I remember the confession, where you had to sort of confess everything was your fault. I think the legacy of the Catholic Church and perhaps all churches is guilt. The concern seems to be with being good, particularly sexually good, rather than helping you find the truth. I remember when I was about seventeen, I began to think, What is this stuff about fire and brimstone? Can we really buy all this – that there's some pit? And shyly asking the new priest, who was a young and attractive man, if he believed in that sort of thing.

My father died when I was 17. Six weeks later my mother lost her mother and she became even more distant. She made me feel stupid and incapable, and I ended up with low self-esteem. About a year after Dad died, I got pregnant. I was very much in love with the man, who married me as a result of my pregnancy. But after my son, my only child, was born, I started to get depressed. Our marriage was very chaotic, and my husband didn't care very much and wanted out. He was never home, and there were tremendous battles. I kept hanging on, hoping that he would shape up, because I loved him a great deal. I was left alone in the apartment day after day, and I couldn't tolerate it. I wanted to go to university and make something of myself. I felt as if I were bricked into a closet and I couldn't breathe. I felt like a child with a child.

My husband was a musician, and when he graduated we moved out to the coast where he got a job. Unbeknownst to me, he had a girlfriend. He walked out a few days before Christmas.

I didn't know one person. There was no one for moral support. I went out and found a job, and I was able to find a little basement suite with no stove, no bathtub and no washing facilities. I had to carry the baby and all his food quite a way to the bus every day, then do his diapers and baby clothes every night after working. I cooked on a hot plate. Those were depressing circumstances.

I carried on like that for nearly a year. I was going downhill all the time. My resources were drained, and I saw no way out of a life of utter deprivation and poverty for Thomas and I. I felt as though I wasn't coping. I felt that I was drowning, that I was putting Thomas on a life raft and hoping for the best.

My husband had always wanted to take Thomas. He was always a better father than husband. I offered to let him take Thomas. That's when the full depression occurred, because I didn't have my son any more. I was trying to go to college to complete a degree to become a teacher. I couldn't concentrate. I couldn't study. I had anxiety attacks. I felt guilty. I felt I deserved this, that what I'd done was terribly unnatural. I gave up my son. What kind of a mother, what kind of a person could I be?

That went on for four years. I was able to hang on, but barely. Eventually I recovered because I met my second husband. He was kind and loving and steady, and he'd just put his arm around me and say everything's going to be okay. He just kept saying that, and eventually it was.

Through all that time, I continued to see my son about every six weeks. I was in Vancouver and they were in Victoria and that was as often as I could afford, financially and emotionally. I would cry for two days before and two days after the visits, because I would feel guilty.

Then I had a second depression three years ago. It's been a long, slow climb, with lots of periods of instability. But since the death of my son, my depression has lifted to a degree. I have more clarity of mind than I have had for three years. I wonder if it isn't a kind of shock therapy. Even the man I live with has noticed the change. I'm not happy, I'm not trying to say that, and the despair and the sorrow are unspeakable. But when they aren't there, I'm more together.

My psychiatrist might say that these things force us to look at what's meaning-ful in life and put things in perspective. That's not what's happening – I always knew what was important. I never loved anybody more than my son. I always knew he was the one who counted most. That's why I've grieved for him ever since he went to his father. Over the past few years we got to be quite close. I really enjoyed our times together, and he stayed here for a month this summer while he worked at a fish plant in Richmond. We had that time together ... I don't think that you're ever the same, you know.

It's hard to think more than one day at a time. If I think much further, I think of the time ahead without him. I wanted to die at first. Sometimes when I feel really swept away, the thought of my eventual death is a consolation. Not because I'm going to meet my Maker, but because I won't have to be aware – it would be an end to the suffering. I've never been suicidal, but when I heard what had happened to my son, as we were driving, I was thinking, "I hope a truck hits us." I wasn't really hoping for it – but these are the thoughts that cross your mind.

For years I felt comfortable with my belief that there wasn't a God, and that what we have is so profound, that life is magical, mystical, metaphysical, that all those things in literature and poetry and art are good enough. My son seemed to feel the same way. I asked him when he was 10, "Well, Thomas, what do you think happens after people die? What do you think is next?" He said, "I think when people are dead they're dead and that's it." And I thought, Well, that's interesting because when I was his age I felt there was a God. I used to say good morning to him on my way to school. This is interesting – he is at the place I am at now. We discussed all kinds of things about life and re-lationships, but not anything theological. I have a good sense that he didn't change too much in those beliefs.

Then when he died – I can't even say it yet – my whole life and beliefs were tossed up in the air, and they're still up there. They've all been challenged. I don't know whether it's because I need support right now, but I'm not ready to believe what I used to believe. It's too overwhelming to think that this is all there is. Right now I'm trying to hang on to, or look at the thought, that there is something else.

The week before he died, I was flipping through a book on biology and looking at the diagram of a cell and thinking, This is amazing. I wonder how this could've come about without there being a creator. I'd never thought that before. Then the thought left me. I thought, Well, that's just fine. Many times since the accident I think about people and the world and all its manifestations and it doesn't seem possible that this creation occurred just because the conditions on the planet were conducive to a blob of protoplasm getting together.

Right now I think there must be something else. Because if there isn't then I've been fooled for a long time about how valuable life is. I can't go back to believing that life is sacred and precious, and feeling the reverence I used to feel for it, if all my son is is that can of ashes in the ground. Because if that's it then it ain't worth it. And yet I see only two options. One is to value life less than I did and put down my reverential, sacred feelings to a quirk of temperament, aesthetic sensibility. Or, I could go and believe in a creator.

Yet maybe there's a third path, where life is as wonderful and mysterious and profound as I thought, and there isn't anything else but this. How much more tragic we are if that's the case. One of the things I liked best about my son was his balance, his grasp of things. I feel I have to live for both of us, in a way. That's all I can do for him.

I went to church a couple of times after he died. The first time I cried all the way through. The second time they were reading about how Jesus could do miracles, and I thought, "Well, if you could do that, then the hell with you." The Christians seem to want to have it both ways. They want you to believe that there's an entity there that hears you, that loves you, that responds to you, but don't expect him to do anything unless maybe he feels like it.

I've gone to Mass a few times. I feel like I'm on a spiritual quest. If my beliefs are challenged, then I have to find out what I believe, what seems to be true. But all I get from the church is more guilt, more rules. I went to see the priest after Mass. He was a man in his late fifties, I guess, and he had been through all the years of philosophy and theological studies. Maybe he was burned out or something. He didn't hear my feelings. He said, "You must be feeling a lot of anger and frustration about the young man's death." I said, "Well, not really, mostly I just feel sorrow." But he kept talking about anger and the frustration. I thought, Well, that's how you feel, and you're not hearing me. And this is supposed to be your business.

Then he wanted to comfort me. He didn't sound foolish or dull or anything, but he was trying to comfort me by saying things like, he believed that when you die your spirit is joined to the Lord in some way, and that all the loneliness and heartache would be gone. I don't feel I'm waiting to be joined with the Lord. If I'm waiting to be rejoined with anybody it's my son. What kind of comfort is that to offer a mother? I'm not interested in that. What concerns me is not my pain, but that my son lost his life. That's what really hurts. It leaves me lost and bereft and inconsolable. The priest's interest was in connecting up with Christ or God. I don't give a shit about that.

I ran a transition house for battered women for three years. Women who came there who had any contact with clergy, it was always bad. The people who helped me spiritually in my life have been people who don't believe in God. They've been people who've been able to look at life, and they're more intelligent, more well read, more compassionate, which is the big thing, and more spiritual than anybody I've ever met from the church. At this moment I'm looking for somewhere to go for some comfort and sense of spirituality, but I don't find it.

I went to a lecture by an astronomy professor who said the great likelihood is that this Earth is the only one of its type. Then he started talking about the un-likelihood of life evolving on the planet simply because conditions were conducive. It helped me look at the question, Was there a creator?

There's a woman at work who believes in God, believes in miracles. But she's very intelligent. We've always talked a lot, but now she has rejected me. She just kind of frosts me out. Yet I know that she was very moved when she found out, but it's as if she can't have her world stirred. I think, Well, religion obviously doesn't make people compassionate, does it? The time you need religion or spiritual comfort the most, it seems to be absent. It makes me feel like starting my own church or something. I met a woman, she came into the office the other day and we just started talking. One thing led to another and she told me her brother had been killed the year before. We've decided to get together and meet and try to do some reading and talking about the nature of the universe, or the nature of God, if there is a God.

Reading the Bible just pisses me off. I don't get past the opening chapters because it's so misogynist I just choke on it. I think, Who wrote this? This is ridiculous. Who is this person? Who says he is divinely inspired? Who says it's the word of Christ? When was it written? I don't know. Who are Mark, John, Peter? What makes them any more inspired than Tolstoy?

Nearly two years later I returned to Vancouver and arranged to have a chat with Nora. I wanted to hear what had happened to her spiritual quest.

I am not as alive this year. When the pain recedes you are left with a sadness and subdued emotions. Everything is quelled a bit. Somehow the spiritual quest got shelved. It didn't get put to rest, it got put aside. I've ceased to read the books I was reading. I've ceased to think a lot about it. I still laugh and enjoy things and plan and get a lot out of things. But there is a feeling of dryness and aloneness.

I joined a Unitarian reading group, really nice people who had come to talk about a variety of issues. What I had on my mind was too intense. I felt uncomfortable – I wasn't interested in discussing what it means to be an ethical person. I went three or four times and felt really discouraged.

Then I went to a funeral for a Red Cross volunteer and there was an Anglican priest. I liked him. I find what is moving for me is the power of someone's belief. Not so much their preaching but just seeing that they are enlivened and strengthened by it. He was talking about Christ. He said that death wasn't the end of life. He said it so plainly and with conviction. I have gone to his church a few times and I really like to listen to him. I must go back more. I don't know why I stopped.

After the first year I remember saying to myself, "It's been a year now, you should be over it." I quit crying. And I rarely cry now. You know the times I cry? After intercourse. I guess it is just letting down the guards and being open. It is still a primitive or elemental sobbing, but it gets all mixed up. It used to be more directly about Thomas. Now it seems to be propelled by other sad things that have happened. I think of all the pain in the world. Someone might live till they are 65, then get cancer, and it takes them five years to die. How do you make sense of that? What kind of a world is this? People are fouled up by their bad childhoods and have to struggle all their lives; people never get off the mat in Africa or wherever. I can't make this into a God-like universe very easily. It can't be that superficial, because people with greater intelligence than mine have had great, firm beliefs. But I'm a sort of stuck in neutral.

I used to think most people were atheists. I was shocked to discover how few people are actually atheists. They are agnostic or uncertain. I would love to believe there is a God – any kind. Just something up there straightening everything out. I don't know if I have thought about what kind. I suppose I go back to what I know about the New Testament and I think about Christ and a loving kind of God. What keeps me from believing? I feel I am on a precipice. It is just the leap, the leap of faith. I don't know what is standing in my way. If there is a God then it's got to be the most powerful thing going. It would touch every aspect of your life. I don't know if I'm ready for that.

AS I LISTEN

Nora's journey was different from the other journeys I heard about, because she was still wandering. She hadn't found anything to anchor or sustain her. A particular event or set of circumstances gave her a real jolt and started her thinking. It started her on a spiritual quest, a quest which is not yet over.

Nora was raised in the church, but then left it. With the death of her son she returned, looking for meaning and resources. But she was disappointed. The church didn't seem to deal with her needs. She needed compassion and understanding. She felt she got dogma and rules.

What impressed me about Nora was her utter integrity. She was on a spiritual quest, and she wanted desperately to believe in a God, but she would not believe unless she could believe with complete honesty. She was an example of a person who puts things to a rigorous intellectual test.

As I heard her story I had the feeling that she represents many people outside the institutional church – and inside it, as well.

AS I RESPOND

"I'm Not Ready to Believe What I Used to Believe"

The tragic death of Nora's 19-year-old son shook her to the roots. Suddenly, what she had believed about life wasn't enough. When she returned to the church, its answers didn't seem to be enough, either. Now she is on a spiritual quest. She is looking for something that will make sense of her son's death, or at least give her strength to bear it.

I experienced something of what Nora went through. I have experienced the sudden death of our daughter at age 21. I have also seen a lot of young men die, men in their early to mid-thirties, at a hospice for people with AIDS. Anyone who tries to make sense of their deaths, anyone who offers comfort too quickly, is trivializing the problem, not solving it.

As I thought about Nora and her struggle to cope with her son's death, I began to think about my own death. There would seem to be little connection between the sudden, accidental death of a young man in full health and the gradually approaching death of a much older person like me. But I am beginning to see a connection, one I should have made long ago. The older I get, the less the age of a person matters, and the more the problem of death does matter. Recently I turned 70. I never thought I would be 70 years old. I never thought I would be an old man. Now I am. I'm supposed to be ready and willing to die any time now, grateful for the many years I've had. But I'm not ready to die, and I wonder why.

Part of it may be that I still fear death, or at least the process of dying, the gradual loss of one's faculties, increased memory loss, increased physical problems, less mobility, failing eyesight or hearing, a narrowing of one's interests, becoming a burden to myself and others. All that I fear and dread.

But there's more than that. I'm enjoying life. In some ways my life is fuller than ever before. Is that the time to die? Perhaps the arguments that made sense to me years ago don't convince me any more. I've learned a lot about life, and I learned a lot of it the hard way. I know things I would never know if I hadn't lived this long. Why can I not begin to use some of that wisdom?

At my age there is no use thinking about getting to the top. You're not considered for most jobs – you're too old. So you ask, "What is so good about getting to the top? Is it worth the effort? What *is* the top?"

You are freed – or forced – to create your own standards; you are not as influenced by public opinion. Gradually you realize it is wonderfully liberating not to have to run around so much. Now, with a pension, modest though it may be, you can choose what you think is important and pursue that. Now, so late in life, you must work out your priorities.

You find you are not so flappable as you were once. Things don't upset you as much – you've been through things like that before. A certain serenity sets in. You can afford to risk your future and your reputation, because there isn't all that much left to lose. Why not spend time doing what you believe in? There is a certain thrill in that. You can afford to be more radical. And life gets simpler in many ways. You see that a lot of intellectual baggage isn't worth carrying around. There are a few simple truths in life, and the rest is commentary.

Nora doesn't appreciate it when a priest tells her to be glad her son is with the Lord. I'm not all that impressed when people tell me life will be so much better in the hereafter. It isn't that I don't believe in a hereafter – I do. But to drag it in as a reason for quitting this life just as it's getting exciting doesn't seem logical. Not at age 70.

Nor am I impressed when people say, "We all have to die, otherwise the planet will become overcrowded." I have no desire to clutter up the planet, and I am willing to make way for somebody else, but it seems to me that having people die when they may just be starting to understand life is a pretty crazy way to solve the problem of overcrowding. I am sure there is something I can do in another life that I can't do here, but why should I go on to that life when there is so much more I want to learn here, and when I may be able to pass on to others some of what I have learned?

A religious person wrote to me after my wife died: "She's the lucky one – she'll see Jesus before we do." That kind of statement infuriates me. My wife had a lot to give here on earth, and she was needed here. It doesn't make sense to say that she died because Jesus wanted her or she wanted Jesus right then.

Nora is challenging some of the statements organized religion has made about life and death, and she encourages me to do the same. Why is death natural? Who says so? Why do we not say, Death is unnatural? Death is evil.

In the book of Genesis we read that the first humans, Adam and Eve, died not because it was God's original plan but as a result of something evil they had done. The clear implication is that God had not included death in the original plan of creation. In the last book of the Bible, when the writer is talking about the last judgment and the sorting out of what is good and what is evil, what is lasting and what will be destroyed, he says, "The last enemy to be destroyed is death."

Nora is on a spiritual quest. She is willing to listen to any words of wisdom people have to offer. In fact, she is hungry for them. But she has to keep her integrity, too. What she accepts must fit her situation. Not even the Bible is sacrosanct. It must address her grief.

Dylan Thomas wrote, "Do not go gentle into that good night ... Rage, rage against the dying of the light." That makes more sense to me than those who speak about the stages of our attitude to death, from denial to acceptance. I'm not denying I am going to die; I am not refusing to accept death.

But I'm not convinced that dumb resignation is wiser or better than raging against the inevitability of death. Wouldn't God see that as a profound appreciation of God's greatest gift of all – life – rather than as the arrogance or immaturity of one who doesn't want to die?

Nora's refusal to accept doctrines just because they are Christian encourages me to question things at a deeper level than I did before. There is something about turning 70 that makes you question what had seemed to be obvious.

When I talked with her two years after her son's death, Nora admitted that in some ways she was farther from God, or less intense in her spiritual quest. Time may be a great healer, but it can also distance us from the situation that made us ask desperate questions.

It's not time that allows me to put off my earnest questioning. It's good health, which can lull me into a false sense of youth. It blurs the advancing birthdays and what they imply. Perhaps hearing Nora's story helped me to raise the question that none of us can really afford to avoid.

Why is there death at all? Why should people die before they have finished their life here? I begin to wonder whether my mistake is in separating life and death, rather than seeing them as parts of a whole. The ancient Hebrews did not believe in a life after death. They believed that the greatest gift of God was a long life on this earth. The Christian church, on the other hand, was born with the resurrection of Jesus. That led the Christians to emphasize life after death. At times the Christian church has downplayed the importance of life on earth. Christians have sometimes regarded our existence here as a mere prelude to the life hereafter. That can trivialize this life. Perhaps that is one of the things I am rebelling against. I don't think this life is only an overture to some distant symphony. Nor do I think it is a bondage to be freed from at death. That is not a worthy picture of this life or the next.

It is possible however, to become so preoccupied with the question of my death that my life can become paralyzed. If I am called to set my mind on God's kingdom and God's justice before everything else, why am I so exercised with the length of my life or the date of my death?

Don't be so anxious about what you will eat, drink or wear, says Jesus. God recognizes that you need such things. But don't let them get in the way of the real purpose of life. Perhaps Jesus could be saying to me, Don't be so taken up with the approach of your death, unjust though it may seem to you. God knows it is an important concern. But don't let it get in the way of the point of your being born. I wonder if my fear of death is related to my attachment to the security of life. Do I fear the risk of the unknown, the disappearance of my security?

I have said age helps to boil life down to a few certainties, and it lets us jettison a lot of speculative baggage. I have said age has helped me learn not to be so flappable about the various crises of life. Why then am I not able to be more relaxed about my approaching death? If I have been able to define what is important in life, define God's kingdom, then what should matter is to be involved in the kingdom. Otherwise I am getting my priorities wrong.

What follows if you set your mind on God's kingdom and justice? "Do not be anxious about tomorrow," Jesus said, "tomorrow will look after itself." I used to think that meant that we should live one day at a time. But Jesus might be saying, Do not be anxious about death or when or why it will happen. That day will look after itself.

That might help to put the matter in its proper perspective. No matter how much I learn or how long I live, the point of my living is to further God's work. God's dream for the world is certainly much larger than I am, and will take many lifetimes to fulfil. The important thing, then, is to be a part of translating that dream into reality in this world – to look for every opportunity to see God's spirit at work in and around us. Jesus said, "Be ready for action ... Be like people who wait for their master's return from a wedding party, ready to let him in the moment he arrives and knocks. Happy are those servants whom the master finds on the alert when he comes" (*Luke 12:35*). What this means to me is, Bet your life – be it long or short – on God's vision for this planet, this universe. Then your way of life and your way of death come together in an all-embracing unity. The big challenge is to risk living for what you believe in.

In one of our conversations, Nora told me that she *wants* to believe in God. "What keeps me from believing?" she asks. "I feel I am on a precipice. It is just the leap, the leap of faith. I don't know what is standing in my way. If there is a God then it's got to be the most powerful thing going. It would touch every aspect of your life. I don't know if I'm ready for that."

When death comes, I want it to catch me in the midst of risking my all for God's vision. Maybe I'm not quite ready for that. Perhaps few people are. I fear being caught spending my time and energy on trivialities. I feel that God understands our fear of taking ultimate risks. And I feel that throughout this struggle, God is struggling with me, as I feel sure God is struggling with Nora.

7
BOB
The Struggle with Homosexuality

Bob is a heavy set man of 41 years. I met him in the office of the AIDS Committee in Saskatoon, Saskatchewan. He is gay. His father died when Bob was 17, and his mother cannot accept his sexual orientation. This situation has left Bob without much immediate support, but he is determined to proceed with his life anyway. He works for a gay magazine and as a volunteer for AIDS Saskatoon as a buddy. A buddy is a friend of a person with AIDS and must be prepared to do almost anything – give moral support and encouragement, prepare meals, run errands, provide basic nursing care, make arrangements for his friend's funeral. Being a buddy can be very demanding. Bob finds satisfaction in his volunteer work but his desire is to become a priest in his church. This request has been denied, and Bob speaks in real pain as a result of that decision.

I was born in Saskatoon 41 years ago. I think I have known I was gay for 20 years, if not longer. It was something I did not deal with well when I first discovered my sexuality. I dealt with it with alcohol. I dealt with it by running away from things. I ran away from a marriage, I ran away from college. When I came out to my family – told them I was gay – I was rejected. I was about twenty-five or twenty-six when I came out to my mother. She totally rejected me and made it impossible for me to communicate with my brothers. The first time the family actually got back together again was four or five years ago. My youngest brother was killed in a motorcycle accident, and that drew the family together. But even then the issue wasn't dealt with. It was like nothing ever happened. Since then my sexuality has never been discussed between my mother and me. We get along half decently well now, as long as the gay subject does not come up. It is never discussed.

I think my mother likes to think I am going to find the right woman and get married and settle down. One of my sisters is a charismatic so she does a lot of praying for me, praying for healing and all sorts of wonderful things like that. I think my other sisters and my brother have accepted the fact that I am gay and I am not going to change.

I have had a real problem dealing with the reaction of my Christian brothers and sisters in the church I go to. I came back to Saskatoon a year ago to attend seminary. I visited with a bishop and talked about his sponsorship. I went before his committee on the ministry and talked about being gay. I talked about my calling and about my Christianity. He was supposed to get in touch with me, but he has never written to me to tell me why I was not accepted. He has never returned any of my calls or answered my letters.

I wonder about my Christianity now, whether I want to be involved in a religion where people don't have the common courtesy to tell you whether you are accepted or give you reasons for not accepting you. I can go to college, but I cannot be ordained without the sponsorship of a bishop. I've sort of pushed Christianity to the back of my life. I was a church-goer, I attended church every Sunday. In the past couple of months I have let it drop. I don't feel comfortable any more going to church. I don't know what I think about religion or Christianity now. I know I have a calling, but I am so angry with the established church and established religion right now that I won't let whatever is inside me come out.

Fifteen years ago I was in the seminary. After I was having problems with my marriage I dropped out. I thought about going back, but it never happened until this year, and then I was turned down.

They talk about accepting people for who they are and accepting people no matter what their sexuality is. They say that as long as you are a non-practising homosexual and you are a Christian, you are acceptable. That I find very irritating. There are too many inconsistencies within the Christian church right now. I don't want to get involved to the point where I could be emotionally damaged again, but I know I need the fellowship, and I want the fellowship. But when it comes Sunday morning, I don't want to be there. I think there are a lot of gay people in the same position.

The woman I married knew I was gay, and it was fine. I said I was bisexual, and I think my wife thought when we got married things would change. They did, for a while. Then I realized I was not getting the affection and companionship I needed as a person. I felt like half a person. I did not feel whole. It was okay with her when I started seeing men again, but then it became a regular thing. She had said she could deal with it, but as things progressed, she discovered she could not deal with my sexuality and deal with the marriage at the same time.

I think I probably hurt her, but I think she knew what she was getting into. I think she knew it might not work, but she was willing to take the chance. Emotionally there was damage on both sides when the marriage broke up. It was difficult. In the past 10 years we have not seen each other or spoken to each other.

I got married to conceal my sexuality. To make my family happy. It was the expected thing to do, I suppose. I know people now wouldn't marry, but I felt I had to. I had to fulfill the expectations of my mother. My mother thinks if I had never gotten married there would have been no questions. The problems started when I got divorced. The reasons for the dissolving of the marriage came out then. If I had decided to stay single, I suppose I would not have had as many problems.

My wife was the second relationship I had. I had had a relationship with a man before the marriage, then after the marriage dissolved, I had a relationship with the man I was with before the marriage. I think each relationship you have gives you insight into people.

For the two and a half years I was married I was not as affectionate as I had been prior to the marriage. Once we were finished with the marriage, I was more affectionate again. It was like I had been suppressing a part of my personality. I loved my wife very much, but as a sister or as a friend, not as a lover. There was not the intimacy I have had in relationships before and since. Maybe I was looking for a female companion, someone to be with, without all the responsibilities of a marriage.

I guess I am out of the closet. If someone asks me if I am gay, I don't deny it. At one time I was radical; I spoke my mind and said I was gay. Now I don't broadcast it. I work in AIDS Saskatoon. I work on a gay magazine. I am open enough to put my name in it, and I sit on the board of directors. I don't go to the gay club but I do attend functions, such as AIDS benefits.

There are still people in our society who don't want to accept us, and some who condemn us to everlasting hell. But I think a lot of people I have met think, "So you're gay, so what," or, "You are just like everybody else." Most of the people I know don't care who I sleep with as long as I perform on my job or am a decent human being.

I am not sure why the church finds it hard to accept me. I would have liked to get a reply from the bishop. There have been problems in Newfoundland with the Roman Catholic priests, and I believe there was an Anglican priest who was involved in a scandal somewhere in Manitoba. I think people in the church are saying, "Fine, as long as you are non-practising." But when they start thinking about the issue, they start to think, "Well, maybe it is not a wise idea even to consider someone for ordination who is homosexual, whether they are practising, non-practising or celibate." I think a lot of bishops and people in charge of congregations and districts are not willing to take on the responsibility of ordaining homosexuals on the chance that the persons may go through, may be ordained, may get a parish, then discover that, yes, their homosexuality is still a very vital part of their life and they cannot be celibate.

We all fight about what the Bible says. The fundamentalists tell us that homosexuality is evil because of Sodom and Gomorrah and a lot of other little things, but when I read the Bible, I can't see where we are condemned. Maybe I have a different edition or something. The thing that comes through to me is Christ, and the love. I don't see Christ condemning people for living their lives the way they feel is necessary. Those people who condemn homosexuality ought to live by all the laws in the Old Testament instead of picking and choosing which laws they feel people have to live by. They condemn homosexuality, but every day they are breaking all sorts of biblical laws.

They make it hard for gay people. That is one of the problems I had with my mother. Because I said I was homosexual I obviously couldn't be Christian, because her version of Christianity, her Bible, tells her that being homosexual is evil. No matter how often I read it, I could never see where she was getting that. My mother is in her sixties and I think it is very hard to change people who have had ideas drilled into their minds for 60 years. I think she accepts me now as a person, and we don't discuss the religious aspects.

I don't think I have ever felt ghettoized or marginalized. When I was living in Calgary, I worked in a gay club and perhaps I was ghettoizing myself. The only people I socialized with were gay people, and I lived in an area that was mainly inhabited by gay people. Then I moved into a suburb and took a different job. People knew I was gay but there was not a problem. I expanded on my relationships and had a lot of straight friends and socialized with them. I think gay people do get ghettoized, but they do it to themselves. I think it is done defensively. It's safer, but it is a very unhealthy way to live.

I think at one point, years ago, I hated myself. For a couple of years I was constantly drunk, but then I realized it was not good for me physically or mentally. So I said, "I love myself and I love who I am. If other people can't handle who and what I am, okay, fine. I will go on and lead my life the way I want to." I suppose it was an unhealthy way of dealing with things. But if I wanted to keep myself from drinking myself into a grave, I had to get on with my life.

You asked me whether my faith has been affected by the attitude and the rejection of the church. I was talking about that with my buddy. He was being a sounding board because I was really angry. We happened to be talking about the church, and he asked me the same question.

At times I guess it has affected my faith. I can't justify that, because I know it is not God's fault. I am angry with the church and not him. But I sometimes feel that God has created the situation in which I am being rejected. Or maybe I have created the situation. I think my faith is probably as strong, but I have had times where I doubted. I have spent a lot of time in the past three or four months trying to figure out what my calling is, and every time I sit down and pray about it and think about it and try to rationalize everything, I think I have been called to minister. Then I have to figure out what kind of ministry I am supposed to have. It has been a real fight.

I feel I have been called to the ordained ministry. Yet am I not ministering now when I visit my buddy and when I do the things that I am doing? That is fulfilling a lot of things for me, but there is still a void. There is still that emptiness. There is still something I have to be doing. It hurts, knowing that I am not doing what I feel I am supposed to be doing, what I feel I have been called to do.

The church committee asked me why I felt I was called. I said I could sit here and say God called me, and I know he did because he spoke to me, but I am not sure *why* I feel it. I mean, it is a gut feeling. It is a *deep, deep* feeling. It is part of me, and I am not sure why it is there. There are days when I get mad at God and I ask, "Why are you putting up all these roadblocks? Is there a reason?" Maybe I am not looking in the right direction. That may be why I was not accepted, because I could not define my calling.

I have a friend in Toronto who has turned in his license and is taking a sabbatical because he is a homosexual. He has been ordained for 12 or 13 years. He couldn't justify being ordained and being a homosexual and not being able to act on his homosexuality. So he has taken some time off. I look at him and I think, "Well, maybe it is best that I am not ordained." But when I say that I feel I'm denying something.

In the meantime, I try to be the person I'm supposed to be. I try to help people. I try to deal with it. It is difficult, because I know that I have a long fight ahead of me. I want to go to university next fall and study and work toward getting my degree. But I also have to try to find a bishop who will ordain me. The one I approached I thought was very liberal. It turned out he is liberal in a lot of senses, but he is extremely conservative in other senses.

I think society will eventually accept gay people. I don't think it is something that will happen in the next 10 years. It is something that is going to take a lot longer. In some churches, it is an issue that has not been dealt with. They know there might be some gay people in their congregation, but as long as they don't know about it, then it is fine. I think what's pushing the issue to the forefront is the United Church. I think if all these people who are professing to be Christians were truly Christians, they wouldn't be dividing and running. They would be coming together and working toward a fulfilling Christian unity, no matter what people's sexuality was.

I think our pastors, our ministers, our priests, no matter how they feel, have to read their Bible and preach it like it is – let the people know that Christ does not condemn homosexuals, that he accepts people for who they are.

I look ahead with hope. I feel things are changing, and I think they are changing positively. It takes a long time, I think. Some gay people are impatient to make a change. But I think eventually we will have a very easy-going society, a place where all of us can live in harmony.

I have never wished that I was not born gay. I am very happy the way I am. If perchance I am never ordained, I feel even now I am fulfilling a portion of my ministry by being involved with AIDS Saskatoon, by having a buddy, by being able to share with people. By just being myself and living the way I live and talking to people. I am not out looking for converts to Christianity, but by the way I live and by my conversation and by the way I deal with people, I think I am showing I am a Christian. If I can help one person be as content in their homosexuality and as happy as I am, then maybe I am fulfilling my ministry already.

AS I LISTEN

Bob was marginalized by his mother and family, and most painfully by his church. But he refused to be ghettoized by society, or to ghettoize himself. It was a constant struggle for him to maintain his self-respect and his faith against the church from which he gained his self-respect and strong faith.

As I listened to him I could not help feeling that he spoke from the bottom of his heart, but also from the depth of his pain. His journey was a struggle of the heart and mind to preserve and to express his faith and to exercise the vocation to which he was sure God has called him.

AS I RESPOND

"I Felt Like Half A Person"

What does it mean to be a complete person? The question haunts and excites me. I respond to Bob with sympathy and understanding because his experience is our experience, his struggle is our struggle. It may not seem to be your struggle if you are not gay, but the very difference of his situation gives him an objectivity and a clarity of insight others may miss simply because they are in the mainstream. By listening to Bob, we see ourselves and our struggles more clearly, and we return to ourselves with more insight.

Bob's feeling of being half a person came when he was married. He realized that he was trying to make himself and his relationship with his wife something that was untrue. The relationship lacked integrity. To have integrity means to be one, a whole, not half a person. Probably the feeling came to Bob before the insight. "I *feel* like half a person. Why do I *feel* that way?" The answer was found in the motivation behind his marriage. "Why did I get married? To conceal my sexuality." Bob dissolved the marriage, even though it hurt him, his wife and his family.

What Bob says to us who want to be whole is that we cannot find wholeness as long as we try to be something others – society, family, church – think we should be. When we do that, we feel discomfort or we feel incomplete. We must examine our motivations. If we accept the standards of others we may be accepted by others, but be rejected by ourselves.

The pressures to conform are great. That is why so many of us reject any part of ourselves we fear society will reject. But doing so, we end up hating ourselves. Bob tried to escape his self-hate by turning to alcohol. There can be no wholeness in such behavior.

When I was a volunteer at a hospice for people with AIDS I found that it was not uncommon for residents to suffer from feelings of guilt or self-rejection.

89

One man went blind with the disease. He said, "This is God's punishment. He has taken away my sight because I lusted with my eyes." In a meeting with a group of relatives of people with AIDS, I found some parents who could not accept the fact that their sons were gay or had AIDS. Some parents felt responsible. Some people say that gay people are bad and that AIDS is the punishment for the sin of homosexuality. The parents may feel condemned. Healing could come only if they accepted their sons and loved them, no matter what others might say.

Bob does not feel he has received acceptance from most of his family. But he has found the courage to accept himself in spite of his family's rejection, the rejection of the church and of much of society. Bob wants a reconciliation with his family, but not at the expense of his integrity.

One man in the hospice for people with AIDS wrote a statement to be read at his funeral. He was the resident who stayed the longest – about nine months. He wrote, "This past year was the best year of my life. I loved my time at the hospice. I have been given the opportunity to approve of myself. To approve of me."

Bob has found some acceptance and support through his faith. He says, "Christ did not condemn homosexuals – he accepts people for who they are." It may sound as though Bob turned from one set of standards – his family, his society, his church – to another – Christ. But Bob has found in Christ someone who is an advocate for him against his detractors, and someone who heals him and makes him feel a whole person. He sees in Christ a savior who is also a healer, who saves him from his self-hatred and who heals the brokenness of his life.

Bob is demonstrating the Old English meaning of the word "health" (haelen), the same word that is used for "wholeness." In Greek, the word "sozo" means both "salvation" and "healing." Healing contains the idea of being restored to what a person was or should be. Bob, I feel, understands this meaning of health and wholeness. It is borne out in the way he has embraced his whole self, including the part that society rejects, and which he rejected from time to time. He also embraces that part of society that rejects him. He is not attracted to a world in which gay people would reject others, and he refuses to be a part of any gay ghetto. He sees his understanding of wholeness as the mission of the Christian church. "We have to work as a complete Christian community," he says. "We should be coming together and working toward Christian unity, no matter what our sexuality is."

From Bob, I gained new incentive to continue my struggle for wholeness, to be a full person. In Bob I see how tempting – and how destructive – it is to be what other people say I should be. The struggle to be complete is so much more important than the struggle to be good or to be right. After all, when Jesus said, "You must be perfect, as your heavenly Father is perfect," he was not talking about moral perfection. He was using the word "perfect" to mean "whole" or "complete." Why love only people who love you? Doesn't everyone do that? Jesus asks us to love our enemies, the people who reject us, and to love the part of ourselves that we reject.

A command to be morally perfect would be impossible to obey. A call to be whole, to be a complete person, on the other hand, is something to which we can all respond. I think Bob has heard that call and that he no longer feels like half a person.

"It Is A Deep Feeling. It Is Part Of Me"

Feeling whole, feeling like a complete person, depends first on finding a way to accept ourselves – all of ourselves. It is a great accomplishment to acknowledge who we are and to try to be that person. But it is not enough to *be* somebody. Most people also feel called to *do* something. Part of being someone of worth is to do something of value. Self-acceptance needs to be followed by a second stage, self-expression.

Bob is expressing himself through his work on a gay magazine and by being a buddy to a person with AIDS. But there is another call he wants to answer – the call to be an ordained minister in his church. Up to now, he has been denied the chance to answer that call. So he rails at the church, he fights against himself, and most of all he fights God.

But the call returns, and Bob is determined to keep knocking at the door of the church. He will not silence the voice within himself. And he will not stop challenging God: "Why are you calling me and then putting up roadblocks?"

Bob's experience is one that many women can identify with. Many women feel called to serve society in occupations that are often denied them because society says, "Those occupations are reserved for men. You don't qualify." To its shame, the church has often not only condoned this repression but promoted it. Many women have felt called, like Bob, to become ordained ministers, but their church has said, "No, this call can't really come from God. God calls only men to be priests or ministers." Yet women continue to have a deep feeling that they are called by God.

It is important that people who hear such cries not sit idly by. To hear a cry that obviously comes from the depths of someone's very being and not respond in a supportive way, is to become part of the roadblock that is put in the person's way. When Bob cries out against God for calling him and then putting obstacles in his way, I hear a call from God to hear Bob's cry and to do something about it.

I heard such a cry some years ago when the editors of a gay magazine in Toronto were taken to court on a charge of using the mails for immoral purposes. The magazine had published an article that seemed to condone pedophilia – men having intimate relationships with boys. But it seemed clear to many of us that the charge was an expression of homophobia and an attempt to punish gay people for the "sin" of homosexuality. I was asked by the magazine to testify in court that, in my opinion, the charge of using the mails for immoral purposes was not justified. I weighed the request carefully. I must admit that I shrank from going. Society had just begun to deal with the issue of gay rights. The congregation of which I was minister was more open-minded than most, but I knew there were many in it who shared society's feelings about gay people. To be honest, I had found the article rather offensive. It would have been easy to decline for that reason.

But something deep within me said, "This request is a cry from an oppressed part of our community. It is a cry for help from people who can only help themselves to a certain degree. Are you not obliged, are you not called, you who enjoy freedom of expression in society, to advocate that freedom for others? Is it not possible that God is calling you as a way of God's response to their cry? How else does God respond than through other people?"

I decided to testify as they had asked. I have never regretted it. Through that action I came, in time, to know and appreciate many gay people in our community and in our congregation. My acquaintance with them broadened my vision and deepened my faith. And I think it added to my perception of what the ministry involves.

We can never be sure that Bob's wish will be fulfilled, at least in the way he perceives it. That may be a great judgment on our society. But society will only be moved to justice by the constant demand for response by people like Bob. Or Bob may be led to some other way of fulfilling his call. After all, he feels some kinship with Jesus, whom he wishes to follow. He must remember how Jesus, who wanted so desperately to lead his people in a way he felt God had called him to lead them, was prevented from doing so. In agony he prayed, "Let this cup pass from me. But if not, let me do your will." Instead of doing what he had set out to do, he ended up on a cross. The Cross has had an effect on the world greater than anything Jesus could have imagined.

Bob has come to the place where he can find some fulfillment in his work on the gay paper and in being a buddy to a person who faces an early death. He has not written off the possibility that something less obvious than the ordained ministry may provide a real way of serving God and people. He says, "If I can help one person be as content in their homosexuality and as happy as I am, then maybe I am fulfilling my ministry already."

8

AUNT BESSIE
The Struggle for Experience

Aunt Bessie is 83 years old and lives with her unmarried son in the tiny fishing village of Pinware, Labrador. Their little cottage looks out on the sea that is the source of their livelihood. It is June, and the wind off the sea is cold, the sun is bright and glistens off the icebergs that float majestically in the distance. The wind whips the clothes on the line outside, while inside the gurgling oil heater warms the kitchen where we sit at the table and talk. Aunt Bessie is a small woman, scarcely five feet tall, and slight. She serves us a bowl of delicious potato and partridge soup, all the while moving and speaking in an animated and energetic way. Her wrinkled face is framed with white hair. She smiles easily and often. She exudes a warmth that transforms the plain little house that is so lacking in amenities into a cosy home.

I was born in Carbonear, Newfoundland, but I came to Labrador when I was 3. My mother married the second time and we had hard times. My stepfather – well, it's just as well for me to tell the truth about it – he wasn't the best to me. He was hard to me and my brother. He was cruel. But he never hit one of his own children. That's what hurt me the most. He wouldn't hit us with his hand. He would take a piece of rope and come right into you. He was really cruel.

I didn't know anything about my real father because he died when I was 9 months old. My stepfather was rough, so I shipped out. I was 11 when I first went out. I went with this old woman and her son, and I washed and scrubbed and mixed bread and worked with the fish and worked in the garden and things like that. I got nine dollars for nine months. She told me I could go to school in the afternoons, but I only did that for three or four days, and then she said, "It's no good to try to work and go to school. You can't do your work if you are going to school." So I had to stay home and work.

Then I decided I was going to come home. My stepfather said, "What are you coming home for?" And I said, "Well, no matter where I go I am not staying there any longer." My brother said, "Come on home, I've got enough fish for you and me." So I went home and I went to school that winter and I got into Grade 2. That spring I shipped out again.

When I was 16, I got married. I got pregnant – I just as well tell the truth – and I married a widower who had two children. It was the days of responsible government, and there wasn't always a lot to eat. Lots of times we had to have bread and molasses and a bit of fish. In the summer it wasn't so bad but in the winter we went on relief – dole it was called then – and we would get six cents a day for each person in the family. That wasn't very much. But we always had our own vegetables from the time I was young until I got too old to grow them.

I've got six children living now, three boys and three girls. I had nine children. My husband was old, older than I was. He died 20 years ago. Our life was pretty rough for the first few years. Oh, but I wouldn't give up. I'm a Newfoundlander – I can't give up! No way. If you've got courage you'll pull up and press on and try.

Forty-two years ago I had lead poisoning. It was poor times then, and there were some shipwrecks up the shore. We got some things out of those shipwrecks. My husband got a galvanized bucket, and I said to him, "Clean that bucket now and if it doesn't do for water it will do for scrubbing, at least." The bucket was painted. Two or three days before Christmas I sat down with the sand and spread out a mat and I started to scrape the paint off it. The next morning I started to feel my chest and I wondered what was wrong but I made the pies and things for Christmas. Christmas Day I got up and there wasn't much to have for the children. We got what we could get and I cooked dinner – cabbage and potatoes and partridges.

I sat down to eat my dinner and I couldn't take it. I just took a nick out of the partridge and I chewed up the bones a little and that was all. After that I took right bad. I was vomiting and sick all the winter up until March. There was a German doctor here then, a woman. She checked me out, then had me go up to the clinic in Fordeaux. The doctor came from Harrington Harbor, Quebec, and he told me that I had lead poisoning.

I realized it was that iron bucket. I had inhaled the steam, you see. So I had my husband condemn the iron kettle and we had to use the tin one. It was no good for a big family, but there was nothing else. In those days you had to wait for the steamer to come down and bring things on it. Now they bring things by plane and truck and all kinds of ways, but you couldn't get things like that then. I weighed 75 pounds when I went in the hospital. I had had all my children by that time.

I had a little girl 4 years old, my youngest. The nurse examined her and said she had a little bit of the poisoning in her gums. She never had a day's sickness from the time she was born until then, but the next winter she got up in the morning and she had her breakfast. She always had her breakfast with her daddy. After her breakfast I went up to make the beds and she said to me, "Mommy, I've got a pain in my tummy. I want to lie down." Then she started to vomit. What she vomited up was just like the yolk of an egg. She vomited again and it was black. She was only 4 years old. She lay on the bed, and every five minutes she'd ask for a drink. I would give her a drink with a spoon - cold water with a little drop of milk in it.

She was like that until six o'clock in the evening. That was the ninth of March. At six o'clock she took a little spell. After that she just opened her eyes and asked for a drink. All night we watched her. At six o'clock in the morning she looked up and she smacked her little hands together and she was gone.

That was my youngest one. I had two dead before her. One fell in the water and then she took paralysis. She was 18 months old. She could run around anywhere. There was a midwife here, down the road, and she got one of those doctor books and looked in it and she said the girl was paralyzed. She never spoke after that. She lived for five days.

The other one that died was a baby. I had the flu and she sucked the breast and she got the flu from me. She was only a month old – she couldn't stand it. Yes, I have had hard times.

I had a dream about my little girl. She would always be playing by herself and talking to herself, but she was a good little girl – never go to bed without saying her prayers. After she died, I had a dream. Certainly I had a vision. After my poor little Margaret died I used to see the other children out playing, and I was always thinking about her. I was sitting in the front window of the house, and I was reading and watching the children out playing and I was thinking about my little girl. I went to bed that night and after I went to sleep I thought I seen our Savior come along by the door and stop right in the doorway – on a little white colt, just as plain as I can see him on that picture up there now. I crumpled my face up and he went around and came back and stood the same way and came back with the sun. When he came back the third time I went out and put my arms about him. Then I woke up. I've often thought about it and I think it was a dream to tell me she was happy. I knew that the three of them was happy then.

Some children are hardened, and it is hard to get them to say their prayers. But not this little girl. From the time she talked until she died she always said her prayers. I often think about her. I think she is safe. I feel her close to me, and when I get over there I hope I will be with her. I do the best I can, and I hope to meet her beyond the pearly gates. It is a blessing to know something like that though, eh? I often think about her.

My marriage was a happy one. They were poor times, but they were happy times. The poor times never made the marriage no worse, because whatever is your lot, you've got to take it. That's what I think. Whatever is going to be is going to be. My husband's children were 9 and 11 when we got married. They were good to me, both my husband's children.

My home was always open. If we only had a cup of tea and some bread and molasses everyone was welcome to it. We always had lots of people around in the poor times as well as the rich times. No one would ever pass the door without coming in, and no one came in and went out without a cup of tea, if it was the last one we had in the house. My husband was the same way. Lots of times I'd see him go and sing out to fellows coming along with their dog teams. "Come in, come in, boy. Come in just for to have a talk and a cup of tea." I think that's a good way. You know – treat your neighbor as yourself.

My stepfather was cruel, and he suffered for it in every way. He went out of his mind in the last three or four years. One spring he got really bad. Someone said to me, "Do you want to go down and see him?" I said, "No, I don't want to go down until he dies, then I'll go to his funeral." But I did go down just the same. You know, I thought it was too bad not to go. I went more for the sake of my mother 'cause she was sick.

I don't know what made him so cruel. I often thought, "If he didn't want us, what did he take us for?" I can remember kicking up a fuss and saying I was going to stay in Carbonear with my grandmother. But my mother said she wasn't going to Labrador without me. Probably if she had known he was going to be so bad to us she would have let me stay in Newfoundland.

What have I learned about life? I don't know. Lots of times children ask me. They come to me and I tell them what I went through. That's my story – what I went through. I went through hard times, and I thank God I'm here yet.

What is God like? God is a spirit. I think God is looking after us, cares for us. When I comes to figure it all out 'tis a mystery and the Bible is a mystery. I can't see very good but I read the Bible. Since I came home from St. Anthony last fall I've read the New Testament right through. I've got a good bit of the Old Testament read but there is a lot of hard words. I read the Bible because it helps me a lot. I think it helps me to get well when I am sick and it helps me to care for others and things like that.

And I pray. I ask God to take care of me and take care of my family and so on. I believe God is close to me. He helps me. I know he do. I've had a lot of sickness and God, he got me through. I've got to 83 years old and I think he has helped me all through life. When I think about my stepfather, no, I am not bitter any more. I speak about it, but I forgets all that now. That's all past and gone and probably he'll suffer for it and probably he won't. I don't know about that. I ask the Lord to forgive him anyway, many times.

I don't have any particular hopes for the rest of my life. I just want to go on and trust in the Lord. I got everything I need now in life, for the time I am here. I suppose I won't be here much longer. But you never know. Only God knows that. I am not afraid of death. I guess you just got to take it as it comes and then after death, the judgment. According to what the Bible says, there will be a judgment. But no, I am not afraid. I suppose I've done things wrong in my life – but there's not many, I think, but do something wrong sometime in their life. The Bible says there is no one perfect, no not one. So, I mean, we've got to believe the Bible, I suppose.

But it is a mystery about the Bible, eh? Now that's a question I've got to ask. 'Tis a mystery. See, there are some things in the Bible will condemn other places in the Bible. Ain't it? Ain't it? So, I mean, 'tis a mystery about it all. I just looks at it. I just reads it over. That's all I can do because I haven't got the education but lots of people tells me I got experience. And experience – lots of times that's as good as education. I'm gifted in my experience, I think. Must be something because I've only got Grade 2, that's all. Never had the privilege to go to school. But if I see a book or something, I'm reading and learning. If I see a hard word, I may not know it but I can sound it out and pronounce it. That's experience, I think. Yep, experience.

AS I LISTEN _____

Aunt Bessie was marginalized geographically because she lived in a remote fishing village in Labrador and socially by her lack of formal education. But in Pinware, Labrador, she was anything but marginalized.

She was an example of how people who may be regarded as marginalized have much to offer the so-called mainstream of society. She lacked many of life's necessities – medical care, proper food – and lost three of her children. But she had an immediate faith that came from her desperate need. She had no formal education but she had experience.

Aunt Bessie was a woman of deep inner strength and remarkable wisdom. She expressed her wisdom in ways that were refreshing and often startling to me.

To meet Aunt Bessie was to immediately warm to her. She poured me a cup of tea and invited me to stay for a drop of potato and partridge soup, and she welcomed me into the warmth of her life without affectation or apology.

AS I RESPOND _____

"I Had A Dream. Certainly I Had A Vision"

It was only natural that Aunt Bessie should dream about her 4-year-old daughter. She never doubted that her Margaret was happy and safe. But she needed to have some assurance that what she believed was true. What she knew in her head needed to be felt in her heart.

Dreams can be a way of making a connection. We all have a certain fund of knowledge or a certain faith, but that knowledge and faith need to be applied to specific situations. Aunt Bessie believed in a God who loves and cares for us. She had experienced that love and care in many situations before. Now she needed to experience them in this situation – the loss of her beloved Margaret, and her feeling of loss and loneliness. The dream helped her to do that. Or, we might say, Aunt Bessie used the dream to make that connection.

Dreams may not provide answers to our problems. They may only express our deep longing for a solution, or they may bring to the surface, to the point of awareness, how real our problem is and how much we need a solution.

Aunt Bessie doesn't seem to have much trouble letting her need surface. But some of us have more inhibitions than she did and we need dreams to release us from them. The cries of our souls are so profound that we tend to silence them for fear that, if uttered, they will destroy us. One of the things we learn as life progresses is that we seldom learn anything we do not need to know. It is out of hunger that we find bread. It is out of our emptiness that we are filled.

The psalms are filled with such paradoxes.

> As the hart longs for flowing streams,
> so longs my soul for thee, O God.
> My soul thirsts for God...
> Why are you cast down, O my soul,
> and why are you disquieted within me?
> Hope in God; for I shall again praise God,
> my help and my God...
> Deep calls to deep at the thunder of thy cataracts;
> all thy waves and thy billows have gone over me.
> By day the Lord commands God's steadfast love;
> and at night God's song is with me,
> a prayer to the God of my life.
>
> *(Psalm 42, selected verses)*

This psalm is an antiphonal prayer in which a needy person cries and God answers. Aunt Bessie uses her dream to create such an antiphon.

Dreams are not the only way in which such connections are made. Dreams may not help some people. But if we allow our soul's deep need to remain near the surface, sooner or later, something rises to respond to it – "deep calls to deep." It may come as we are reading a book. Suddenly a line leaps off the page and strikes a responsive chord within us. The line may come quite out of context, but it makes the connection with our need. Or it may come in listening to music. The music articulates and replies in a language the heart understands. However it happens, it is not a passive experience. We must embrace and appropriate the response when it comes. Otherwise the dream or the line or the music is lost.

Aunt Bessie knew, after her dream, that little Margaret and her other two children who had died were happy and safe. That was enough. Perhaps it is significant that the knowledge came as she put her arms around her Savior. She did not blame the Savior for the loss of her child. He came as a friend who understood and cared, not as an enemy.

That did not take away the mystery of how a just and loving God could countenance the tragic death of a beautiful 4-year-old child. But the dream moved it beyond explanations and answers to another context. It helped Aunt Bessie to make the connection between her pain and the spiritual healing that was offered. The dream helped her to appropriate what she knew to be true and to apply it to herself. "I hope to meet her beyond the pearly gates. It is a blessing to know something like that."

"'Tis A Mystery About The Bible"

Aunt Bessie noticed contradictions in the Bible. She had innocently put her finger on a question that has tormented ordinary Christians and learned scholars for centuries. How to resolve the contradictions in the Bible? People have used these contradictions to line up on opposite sides of many issues: capital punishment, peace and war, abortion, homosexuality, the place of women. Aunt Bessie believes that if she had more education she might resolve these contradictions. Alas, more education only seems to emphasize the contradictions and to intensify the debate. Aunt Bessie seems to rise above such debate.

Aunt Bessie reads the Bible not to try to resolve its contradictions but, as she says, "because it helps me a lot. I think it helps me to get well when I am sick and it helps me to care for others."

She doesn't rely solely on the Bible for her wisdom. She blends the healing and guidance she gets from the Bible with the knowledge and insight she gets from her own experience. Aunt Bessie has been through a lot – hard times, sickness, the death of her husband and three of her children. She has a wealth of experience. She reminds me of a powerful verse in Paul's letter to the Romans: "Tribulation worketh patience, and patience experience, and experience hope." I found that the original Greek word that is used for "experience" comes from a word which means "to test, examine, prove, scrutinize." In other words, to see whether a thing be genuine or not.

That, I think, is what Aunt Bessie means by experience. She regards it as a gift. It is a special ability God gives to humans that endows us with a kind of transcendence. Some people are able to get above the things that happen to them – things like suffering. I can become so completely absorbed in my suffering that I have no way of assessing its meaning or coping with it. I need to get above it so I can look at it, see it in a larger context, put it to some kind of test. Experience is rising out of the event or feeling of the moment in order to name it for what it is and ascribe a meaning to it.

That is what the Bible is all about. It is a book of experience. It is a record of events, and of the meanings people ascribed to those events – events they had been through or witnessed. The Hebrews escaped from bondage in Egypt. They came to believe that the escape was part of a plan of God to free them from slavery and to lead them to a Promised Land. On that "experience" they built a great deal of their faith in a God who would deliver them from whatever bondage they might be in.

The meanings and interpretations people find in events will differ – according to people's interests and limitations, according to the times and places in which they live, according to their cultures. That is why some things in the Bible will contradict other things in the Bible. People have attached different meanings to the same sayings, ascribed different characteristics to the same God, developed different standards to live by while claiming to be guided by the same commandments. That ought not to be surprising. Only if we see the Bible as a book dictated by God, using human beings only as scribes, could there be only one meaning. But if the Bible is a book dictated by God, we can't put it to the test of our experience. We must be passively obedient to whatever the Bible says. Except, of course, that people cannot agree on what it says.

What is the solution? It is to see the Bible as a marvellous record of God's experience with people and of people's experience with God. It is to see the Bible as part of the ongoing phenomenon of the human race. Anything that is ongoing is alive and growing. That is why Jesus can say: "You have heard how it has been said, 'An eye for an eye and a tooth for a tooth,' but I say to you, 'Do not resist one who is evil. But if one strikes you on the right cheek, turn to them the other also ... and if anyone forces you to go one mile, go with them two miles.'"

Jesus is obviously not afraid to improve on old standards. How have he and others come to improve on the experience they have received from former generations? By comparing it with their own experiences and by constantly testing all experiences by their growing understanding of God.

Jesus calls us to constantly reassess, with God's guidance, the meaning of events and the implications of standards we have set. The implication is that God is a dynamic God, a living God, as the Bible so often says, and that this living God is constantly showing us more and more truths. We call that "progressive revelation," and with it goes "progressive interpretation."

Aunt Bessie tries to assess her stepfather's cruelty to her. Years later, she prays to God to forgive him, and tries to do so herself. When she can't quite bring herself to forgive him she tries to forget his cruelty. Putting her feelings to the test, she finds she is not happy with them. She decides to apply different standards, and finds she can feel mercy. As she prays, she feels she is not condemned by God. She comes up with a new wisdom.

Experience is ongoing and dynamic, something like the Bible. We keep growing in our understanding of God, of people, of life and of ourselves.

People who trust their own experience read the Bible with enlightened eyes. They arrive at a deeper, fuller faith than do people who read the Bible as if experience somehow stops at a certain point, and there is nothing left to learn. That approach does violence to the Bible as a record of ongoing experience. It also ignores or demeans what God can teach us through our experience.

Aunt Bessie helps me read the Bible with a new appreciation and freedom. Yes, as Aunt Bessie says, there are contradictions in the Bible. They perplex me and confuse me. But I am no longer surprised by them. Instead, I am challenged, as writers of the Bible were, to learn from others' experience and to build on it. I am also encouraged to trust that the God who used other people's experience can also use mine. Given the wide variety of human experience, just how all that is done is, as Aunt Bessie says, "a mystery."

CONCLUSION
Struggle and Faith

Many years ago I travelled with a friend to Africa. We spoke with many people as we tried to understand the developments in their countries. I will never forget talking with the minister of information in Lagos, Nigeria. I asked him about their form of government, a one-party democracy. I asked how a one-party system could be described as a democracy. He replied that democracy is a concept that has to be worked out according to the culture and history of each society. He asked me if democracy in Canada was the pure Athenian type. He described the tribal traditions of his country and how the chief, after consulting the elders, would make his decision. That, he said, is the background we must remember when we initiate parliamentary democracy. That is why it is a one-party system. I returned home with a broader and deeper understanding of democracy and I examined and questioned our own government with a new objectivity.

I feel somewhat the same after this journey to a variety of people. After listening to their stories, I return to my own with a new objectivity and with insights I did not have before. I am aware that their stories and mine are not just individual stories, although each one is different and unique. They are part of the human story. Each one enlightens and illustrates the human story, and their individual stories are, in turn, enhanced and better understood in the light of the whole human story.

As I went over them, certain themes seemed to recur, themes that run through the lives of most people in one way or another. There is the struggle with their past, especially with their childhood. There is the question of where and how they got their values. Many of them suffered violence or participated in violence of one sort or another. There was an incredible amount of suffering, physical, emotional and spiritual. Many of them experienced an important turning point in their lives, something like a conversion. Some were faced with the problem of how to forgive some form of cruelty they had experienced. And all of them struggled to arrive at some form of belief or faith.

While each of these themes has filled many large books, it might be helpful if they could now be considered in the light of what the people who told us their stories discovered about them. Precisely because they often speak from a different perspective than many of us, these people have insights that may have escaped us and from which we might learn.

Let us think about the struggle with our childhood. We are all aware, sometimes painfully, of how profound an effect our early years have on us. It is a part of our lives over which we have little or no control while it is happening. We have no say as to where or when we will be born; we can't decide who will be our parents. Some people, like Don, don't know who their parents are. Don talks about how that affected him. He was shunted from foster home to foster home for the first eight years of his life. That made him a transient for the rest of it. Don says he spent his early years trying to figure out what was going to happen to him, rather than learning the elementary lessons of life. He was constantly hungry for love.

Lorne would wait up at night for his parents, afraid they might drown as they crossed the river to get home. At school he was harassed by the other children because of his race and got no support from the principal. Marlene was sexually abused for most of her childhood and didn't know that her stepfather was not her real father until she was 17. For years she had to suffer from the rejection of her friends because her stepfather was a bootlegger. And when she got pregnant as a teenager and the child turned out to be mentally handicapped, her mother told her that was the punishment of God. Donna's mother had a violent streak; she destroyed Donna's pet dogs. Donna's older brother raped her. Aunt Bessie was cruelly beaten by her stepfather and chose to leave home.

How did they survive? There is no doubt these people suffered, but none of them became mere products of their childhood. They all found ways to rise above their childhood – to transcend it. At some point each decided not to be a victim of the past but to be a shaper of it. That is, they discovered within themselves an inherent creativity, something all human beings are given because they are the children of a God who is by nature a creator. Their creativity allowed these people to take the material they were given – their painful childhoods – and make something out of it, something useful and beautiful.

It took a lot of courage to do that, and a lot of faith. It meant believing something about themselves quite contrary to what their childhoods taught them. Tentatively at first, then more confidently as they proved themselves, they moved out of their cramping and distorted shells. They grew. They put some distance between themselves and their early years and gained sufficient perspective to see what might be of value from their childhoods and to salvage it. Then they rejected the destructive parts or used them to better understand other people who had had difficult childhoods.

I am a child of the Depression and I have many times been aware of how that has affected me. Because of the poverty that struck us all, I became very cautious about money, and about taking risks. Because my father was attracted to a particular kind of religion during that period, and because I was at an age when I was affected by his influence, I began my religious pilgrimage as a fundamentalist Christian. For both of these influences I have been grateful. Poverty taught me thrift and gratitude for simple blessings. Fundamentalist Christianity taught me a love for the Bible and the importance of personal commitment to God. But precisely because the blessings were mixed blessings, I had to struggle to sort out the good from the bad. While honouring the blessings of thrift and caution, I had to try to learn the excitement of risk. I had to learn the value of spending my all on something I perceived to be of real value – like Jesus' story of the man who sold all he had to buy the pearl of great price. I appreciated the gifts of a fundamentalist faith, but I had to struggle with the narrowness that would exclude all but a few from the kingdom of God, and that stifled the movement of the Holy Spirit by dictating too narrowly just what the life of a Christian means.

When we try to get beyond our upbringing we feel guilty. We feel we are disobeying our parents – the authority figures. That is why Marlene is such an inspiration to me. Here is a person who has been told by everyone that she is no good. Yet she risks believing people when they ask her to take on a new responsibility. She must disobey the people she had assumed knew best. She must choose a new kind of God.

We all know we can't choose our parents. And yet there came a time in the life of Marlene and Donna and the others when they did choose their parents. That is, they chose their authority figures. That is the mark of maturity. We cease being helpless victims of our past and become the designers of our future. As I look at the amazing achievements of these people I am challenged, by the grace of God, to believe it is never too late to design my future.

Choosing our own authority figures helps us to choose our own values and make our own judgments. We have no control over the cultural values we grow up with. All too easily we assume they are the right values, the right judgments. But in time we may begin to see that they are stereotypes.

Marlene suffered from the stereotype her social workers taught her of welfare people – that they were lazy, dirty, unable to manage money, cheaters and that they had dubious morals. Don knew there was a stigma against street people and anyone who didn't hold a regular job. Donna lashed out at urbanites who looked down on hookers and homeless people. Lorne felt the pain of racial discrimination – Indians were not as good as white people. Bob experienced the rejection of his family and church because he was gay.

We are conditioned to believe that society knows best. That is why it is so hard to choose our own values. We must move from the majority to the minority – sometimes a minority of one! And there is no guarantee that the values we choose will be any better than the values we rejected.

First we must evaluate the values we have accepted without question. How do we do that? By trusting our own experience. Bob, told by parents and church that it was a sin to be gay, tried to conform to their judgment. He got married. It didn't work. He felt like half a person. He read the life of Jesus, he felt deeply that he was accepted by this Christ. Bob tested his inner feelings against what he felt to be a higher standard than the standard of his mother and his church. He threw off their judgments. It took courage. It was a risk. He could be wrong. But he believed it was the right decision.

I used to feel that if I questioned a value or a judgment dictated by others, I was duty bound to offer an alternative. But as I think of the stories of these people, I realize that many of them did not know what standard they were going to choose when they rejected an old one. The first step was to say no to something they could not, with integrity, accept. Then they were free to search for something better, something they would choose, not merely accept, something they might have a part in creating. Donna, after rejecting the standards of her parents and the judgments of society wandered in a moral wilderness for a while before she found a real alternative. But the rejection of the old set her free to search for the new.

The worst stereotype is the image we have of ourselves. Jennifer spoke of how her depression made her feel that she was a worthless human being, that there was no point in fighting her illness any longer. In her brief moments of health, she knew she was a creation of God, made in the image of God. Does God make ugly, worthless beings? Does a master artist create trash? Does a great composer make noise? Can a God of infinite love and artistry make anything other than a person of infinite beauty and worth? Could she risk believing she was beautiful and worthy? Miracle of miracles, she did. And she encouraged me to believe I was a person of value on those many occasions when I suffered from low self-esteem, a stereotype that so many people seem to accept about themselves for no apparent reason. Finding a way to break the hold of a false image we have of ourselves seems to be the key to finding a way to break the hold of the false images we have of others.

The handicaps imposed on many of these people by their unhappy child-hoods and by their legacy of distorted values were experienced in their most extreme form in acts of violence. The amount of violence, physical, emotional and spiritual, these people sustained is beyond the experience of many of us. Marlene was sexually abused throughout her childhood, was kept as a slave by her husband, forbidden to leave the house, battered, then finally aban-doned. Donna was raped by her brother and threatened with a gun by her mother. Aunt Bessie was beaten regularly with a rope by her stepfather and sent away at a tender age to work for a dollar a month for a woman who wouldn't let her to go to school.

Violence seems to become a way of life for many of these people. Don got into fights to prove himself, and to try to express his loneliness and rage at being rejected by society. Lorne blew up at a trial where he was ordered to pay support for another man's child.

But all of these people renounce violence as a way of life. It is important for us to learn how they did it, because our violence is so much more subtle and controlled that it is often overlooked. It comes out in such forms as hostile take-overs in business, back-stabbing in politics, and cutting remarks in many a relationship.

Don's insight into the cause of violence is the one I find most helpful. People fight, he says, when there is a big hole in their lives – when they feel they don't belong anywhere or to anyone and when they have lost all their self-respect. People have a need to express themselves, and if they can't do it construc-tively they will do it destructively. Not belonging means not being needed or appreciated. People need to be told there is a God, that this is God's world, and that all people have a right to be here.

That insight rings true for me. I know how children can throw temper tantrums when their parents are entertaining guests. The children feel excluded. Sud-denly, they don't belong. They are told to be quiet. They erupt in some kind of violence. The wise parent finds a way to recognize the children, to include them, without letting them dominate.

Don helps us understand some of the violence we see on our streets. An un-employed man, for example, feels cut off from society, as though he has nothing to contribute. He has no way to express himself constructively so he lashes out, fights, steals, even murders. Often such behavior is simply punished, and the man is locked behind bars. He is further excluded. We need to examine the hole in the middle of his life and ask how it can be filled.

In these stories, there was suffering that came from events over which no one had any control. I am thinking of the birth of Marlene's handicapped child, of Jennifer's depression, of the deaths of Nora's son and Aunt Bessie's children. I experienced similar events in my life, and I felt especially drawn to the suffering of these people.

I can identify with the kind of gradual progress Marlene made in her acceptance of her mentally handicapped child. First she had to get rid of the guilt her mother imposed on her – that God was punishing her for getting pregnant before she was married. Marlene believed in a loving and caring God. She knew a loving and caring God would not do that. She started praying hard for a big miracle that would cure her son. It didn't happen. So she learned to be grateful for little miracles, like a medication that reduced her son's seizures. Then she began to see how she could use her misfortune for good. She was asked to work in a center for handicapped people. The people she worked with taught her to give her own son more responsibility, not to keep him dependent. They showered her with love, and they appreciated her love for them. Marlene learned to live with the mystery of life. Because Marlene's pilgrimage parallels much of my own experience with our handicapped child, her pilgrimage confirms and strengthens my experience.

Jennifer's long fight with depression moves me most deeply. Her depression caused so many kinds of suffering in addition to the pain of being depressed. There is the loss of perspective. Jennifer feels that she is a worthless individual, that she is somehow responsible for her own depression. There is the frustration of not being able to do anything about it. There is the feeling of powerlessness. There is anger against God for allowing this to happen. There is an incredible loneliness.

Yet Jennifer does not surrender to her suffering. Paradoxically, in the midst of feeling that God has abandoned her, she feels close to God. Nora cannot say that God is closer to her in her suffering, but she feels a certain sense of the sacredness of her suffering, something that starts her on a spiritual quest. In the experience of the deaths of my wife and my daughter I mysteriously felt the presence of God in a way I had never felt it before.

Jennifer uses her suffering creatively, an incredible achievement when we think of how incapacitating her suffering is. She saw her ongoing suffering as a journey. I thought about my wife's depression and what it did to her and to me. Pain brings you face to face with a very harsh reality. You never forget that, but as you look back, you see how your pain can make you more sensitive and understanding of others who are going through the same thing.

Some good things happen to the people in these stories. Many of them reached a turning point in their lives, a point where *things* don't necessarily get any better but the people do. It doesn't happen from the outside, it happens from the inside. Call it a conversion, if you like.

Marlene, at the depths of feelings of worthlessness, living on welfare, abandoned by her husband, is offered a job. It is a crucial moment. Should she take it or remain in the security of the hated welfare? She takes it. And she is changed from a dependent to an independent person.

Jennifer decides to make a journey out of her depression, rather than accepting it as the end of the road. Bob decides not to flee from his self-hate and the judgment of his family and church any longer. He turns from alcohol, and learns to accept himself for who he is.

Lorne, after a long search and many bouts of alcoholism, went humbly into a sweat lodge and emerged a different person. Donna rebelled against her parents and society and made herself into a kind of social parasite. After the suicide of her best buddy she is never the same again.

None of these people changed because somebody told them to. But they all felt a desperate *need* to change. They were disillusioned with the life they were living. They could not go on. Something had to change. *They* had to change.

We could call this creative disillusionment. The end of one way of life can lead to another way – a better and different way. These people took some kind of symbolic action. Marlene takes the job that is offered. Bob decides he can live without his mother's approval. Lorne starts to say "Thank you" and "I'm sorry." Donna takes home her friend's cat.

But because these actions are symbolic, they take a great deal of faith and courage. Often people believe they can take these steps only with the help of God – that God leads them to take the steps. Other people say their conversion comes without reference to God or recognizable religious helps; it comes with the help of loving and supportive people, and it comes with a lot of heart-searching.

It is wrong to try to limit the action of the Spirit to certain words or categories or concepts. That is a kind of stereotyping of the Spirit that is as stifling as the stereotyping of races or classes. Christians have long since learned that they have no monopoly on the Spirit. They know that the Spirit is at work in all the great world religions. Donna teaches us that the Spirit is also at work outside any organized religion, too. Just as one religion can learn from another, so all religions can learn from people they might call non-religious. As Don put it, everybody is religious in one way or another.

After the turning point in their lives, many of these people tried to forgive the people who had hurt them. Marlene and Aunt Bessie had to try to forgive their stepfathers. Lorne had to try to forgive his wife. But it isn't easy to forgive people who have hurt us. Aunt Bessie still finds it hard to forgive her stepfather. Forgiveness is hard for all of us because it seems to trivialize both the seriousness of the injury that was done and the hurt we feel. It seems unjust. People should pay for what they do. That is the basis of our justice system. It is also the basis of our work ethic. People should earn what they get and get what they earn. To forgive someone seems like paying them a salary for nothing or like giving them something they want without asking them to pay for it.

But some things are simply beyond payment. What Marlene's stepfather and husband did to her could not be remedied by any amount of payment or punishment. The deep hurt Aunt Bessie felt could not be made up for. The magnitude of the hurt and the seriousness of the misdeed could only be acknowledged by an act of forgiveness.

Lorne does not wait for his wife to repent of her deeds and to ask for his forgiveness. Instead, he takes the initiative. He decides "to make an amend."

This brings a new dimension to forgiveness. The real tragedy is not always the misdeeds of others but the break in our relationships. I do not want to be a victim of an evil action – I want to do something creative about it. Was I in any way responsible for the evil action? If so, I can do something about that. If not, and if no reconciliation is possible, there may be constructive things that can be done to improve the situation. In the end, I must deal with what the experience has done to me. No one can do that for me. I have to keep my integrity. I have to act in a way that preserves my self-respect. Above all, I must become an active agent instead of a passive victim. Lorne said the same thing with

111

actions rather than words. If I adopt this approach, there will be less argument about why and under what conditions I should forgive. I will simply forgive as a way of life. The people in these stories are survivors. They survived childhood abuse, cultural prejudices, misfortunes, violence. But they are more than survivors. They experienced major changes in their lives. They have learned to forgive and to be forgiven. They have progressed from being survivors to becoming believers.

Theirs is not a formal faith, not a set of beliefs. It is not a collection of opinions they hold. Their faith is a way of coping with specific situations and making some sense of them. They have discovered certain resources within and beyond themselves, and decided to live in certain ways – ways different from how they lived before. Their faith is not something they can prove by intellectual arguments – it is something they have proved in the fires of their own struggles.

Because they are different people and because their situations are different, their faith is expressed in different ways. Marlene has faith that she is loved and cared for, perhaps even more than she loves and cares for her own children. She has faith that God has brought her this far and will help her through the future. It is a faith that can afford to leave some things unexplained, like the handicap of her son, because Marlene can endure even those things she cannot understand.

Don has faith that he belongs in this world, even though it seems to reject him, because it is God's world. He has a contribution to make to this world, and his contribution will be accepted and appreciated. His faith assures him that he is a giver and not just a taker. As for the future, he is not certain, but he feels that he can "trust the music" and trust the feelings to keep him on track.

Donna believes in the kind of love that Beth and her other friends demonstrate. It is a love that, while it has certain expectations and makes certain demands, is ultimately unconditional.

Jennifer dares to hope and to keep on hoping in the face of a seemingly incurable illness. Even if she never recovers from the illness, she can use her pain to make her a better person. She has faith that, when she feels most alone, God is nearest.

Lorne's faith is the source of his spirituality. His faith was an anchor for him when he was drifting and being driven to personal destruction. Because of his faith, he was able to accept a self he had always rejected, to accept himself as Lorne, as an Indian and as an alcoholic. He can approach God without shame or fear. There is "no need to cringe."

Faith is something that seems to elude Nora, but she knows what she is searching for. She wants to believe there is a God who is interested in her and in her suffering, a God of compassion. She feels the need for a God who will give some meaning to the universe and provide her with a way to understand tragedy. There are times when she is on the verge of believing in that kind of God but she hesitates because she is not sure she could respond with the total commitment such a faith requires.

Bob has faith that whatever he feels deeply, especially when that feeling refuses to go away, must be heeded as the voice of God. For him the voice says, "I love you and accept you for what you are, as a homosexual. And I call you to serve in my church."

Aunt Bessie believes there is a God who helps her through hardships, who heals her when she's sick and helps her treat others better. God cares for her and her loved ones here and in the hereafter. Such things she feels confident about because of her gift of experience.

The faith of these people rings true for me. Whatever faith I have must be constantly put to the test – in the way I live, the priorities I make, the way I treat people, the time and energy I give to prayer, meditation and service to others. My faith should make me a person of hope and a person who gives hope to others. I, too, have been through some fires of testing and I, too, have experienced that God is loving and God is strong.

There are other, very different, faiths all around us which we have, perhaps unconsciously, accepted and lived by. Think of the people in these stories. Why did they have to struggle? Why did it take them so long to come to their new faith? Was it not because they had been living by another faith? Marlene was told she was a sinner in the eyes of God. She was told she was a creature of no worth by her mother and by her husband, and she believed it. Perhaps they did, too. Her faith in their judgment crippled her emotionally and spiritually.

Jennifer, when she was depressed, was the captive of a faith that told her she must be responsible for her illness. Some medical people said she was suffering from a kind of learned helplessness. Society said she was unemployable;

the university said she did not fit the system; other people said she should be institutionalized. All those opinions became a kind of perverted faith that led to despair rather than hope.

Donna had to battle a doctrine that said the dice were loaded against her, and that she should make life miserable for the people who loaded the dice. Donna led a life of irresponsibility. She felt a despair that made her take overdoses of drugs that could have been fatal. She never thought she would live to the age of 30.

Lorne and Bob were taught to believe they were inferior, Lorne because of his race, Bob because of his sexual orientation. No one can live on a faith like that. They both made ill-advised marriages and took to drink.

Nora was raised to believe that God is a God of rigid rules, mostly rules about a person's sex life, and that God is more interested in making sure a person believes the right things than in helping a person who is suffering or searching. For now, at least, she would rather be an atheist or an agnostic.

Who is responsible for such malicious doctrines and for the havoc they wreak? Religion must take its share of responsibility, for some of these beliefs have been taught in the name of religion. But society is also responsible. Society preaches daily, especially in advertisements. The advertisements tell us things like, "You must get to the top. Here's the way to do it." Or, "We know you want to look beautiful and be attractive. That means you must stay young-looking. We'll help you. Buy our cosmetic, or enter our course in dieting or exercising."

The advertisers would have us believe that we are things, not persons. Things to be manipulated. Things to be changed and improved from the outside, by external forces. We are urged to eat this, drink that, wear this, apply that, drive this. If we stop to think, we realize that we are not being valued for who we are – we are only valued as consumers of certain products.

Advertising denies that we are human beings who are born to be creators, co-creators with God. The secular gospel says that we are not creators; we are at best reactors, or objects of fate and of the advertisers' products. The products will remake us.

We buy their advice because it is tempting to believe that we can be transformed without having to change. We can purchase what we cannot do. Part of our acceptance of the advertising message comes from our low self-esteem. And why would our esteem not be low as long as secular and religious authorities imply we are sinful people – or not even people but things?

The people who told these stories were tempted and influenced by many forces. But they dared to listen to another voice, an inner voice that said, "Stop listening to these doctrines. They do not really care about you. Listen to the voice that says you were created in the image of God, endowed with beauty and goodness and worth. Believe that voice. Trust it. Risk acting as if it were true. You will not be left on your own. You will receive strength as you need it. If you fall, you will be forgiven and helped to get up and try again. Perhaps life has dealt you a poor hand. Let us see what we can do with it. You may well be in for a delightful surprise."

That is the sort of thing I hear these people saying, by the way they live and by the way they speak. Nobody told them to say it. They are telling about their own experience. They have tested it and found it to be true. Their experience is the outcome of their intensely human struggle.

That is why their faith speaks to me so powerfully. It seems to come from someplace very deep, and it speaks to someplace very deep within me. It sets up a resonance within me, inspires a sublime conversation. And somewhere in the conversation I sense that we are not alone. Someone Else has joined us. Someone Else is listening. Yes, and more than listening. I sense that this conversation is not just between us. Someone has entered into the conversation. In fact, I begin to feel that this Someone started the conversation. From the depths of the universe, a sound has gone forth and struck a chord in the depths of our souls.